Rethinking Classroom Participation

Listening to Silent Voices

Katherine Schultz

foreword by
Ray McDermott

Teachers College
Columbia University
New York and London

Published by Teachers College Press, 1234 Amsterdam Avenue, New York, NY 10027

The author wishes to acknowledge use from the following works:

"A Litany for Survival," from *The Black Unicorn*, by Audre Lorde. Copyright © 1978 by Audre Lorde. Used by permission of W. W. Norton & Company, Inc.

"Cartographies of Silence," from *The Fact of a Doorframe: Selected Poems, 1950–2001*, by Adrienne Rich. Copyright © 2002 by Adrienne Rich. Used by permission of the author and W. W. Norton & Company, Inc.

Library of Congress Cataloging-in-Publication Data

Schultz, Katherine.
   Rethinking classroom participation : listening to silent voices / Katherine Schultz ; foreword by Ray McDermott.
      p. cm.
   Includes bibliographical references and index.
   ISBN 978-0-8077-5017-9 (pbk. : alk. paper) — ISBN 978-0-8077-5018-6 (hardcover : alk. paper) 1. Classroom management. 2. Self-esteem in children. 3. Educational psychology. 4. Silence. I. Title.

   LB3013.S38 2009
   371.102'4—dc22

                                                                    2009024931

ISBN: 978-0-8077-5017-9 (paperback)
ISBN: 978-0-8077-5018-6 (hardcover)

Printed on acid-free paper

Manufactured in the United States of America

16 15 14 13 12 11 10 09   8 7 6 5 4 3 2 1

Rethinking
Classroom Participation

To my father, Franklin Morton Schultz, who at 91, through silence and speech, continues to be one of the most supportive people I can imagine.

In memory of Marci Resnick, who worked tirelessly to make the world a better place, and whose constant questioning, love, and silent attention continue to inspire my work.

Contents

Foreword:
Silence in High Relief

A YOUNG WILLIAM BUTLER YEATS mourned the passing of an older time when the deeds of "warring kings"—those "word be-mockers"—filled the world. Their glories long gone get now reduced to only "an idle word . . . [b]y the stammering schoolboy said/Reading some entangled story." We in our turn are also struck and stuck with idle words, encouraged only by the shaky promise that "words alone are certain good." In circumstances of our own making, with right words of our own choosing, we just might reorder the world. Words can make a difference, said Yeats, for "The wandering earth herself may be/Only a sudden flaming word" (1889/1983).

Teachers are charged to change the world. So what's with the language of "the stammering schoolboy": borrowed words recited at center stage, fluency and ingenuity mumbled in corner outrage, teachers hammering and children stammering. Why not "a sudden flaming word" in school? Why not some appreciation for the sudden flaming wisdom of children from those word be-*machas* (the Yiddish for word be-big shots), for children ever ready to say what has to be said, if only their adults would listen?

Enter Katherine Schultz, urging teachers to make the most of what children in classrooms do not say, cannot say, are not allowed to say, do not have the opportunity to say. Schultz thinks children should have more room for spoken and written expression, of course, but her main excitement is that teachers must appreciate as well the wisdom held back, hidden, alienated, and cried out in silence. Neither talk nor silence guarantees learning. They are both better understood as forms of engagement and participation that contribute to learning in proportions every teacher must worry about and rework by the moment. Words can make a difference, says Schultz, particularly if teachers listen to the silence that surrounds them, makes them sudden, and gives them flame. We need teachers—those word be-*machos*, chest-beating rule-bleating authority figures always with the last word—to try a little silence of their own and to recognize the sudden flaming silence of children judging, juggling, appropriating, and disrupting the presumptions of adults.

A critic praised Samuel Beckett's *Waiting for Godot* as a play in two acts, a play in which "nothing happens, twice" (Mercier, 1977). Silence can play to a full house, most famously in Native American cultures, most elaborately in Japanese theater (with Noh words); even Shakespeare, with all those words, all that noise, had to tap the seductions of silence (Gross, 2001); and Harold Pinter followed Beckett in raising them to central focus. Silence can dominate a scene and have its say—and more than its say. Silence can also be the key to the system. Schultz keys on five functions of silence in classrooms: resistance, reluctance, assertion, protection, and reflection. Important business, these functions of silence, and good teachers must learn to work with them (McDermott, 2005).

Schultz names other kinds of silence as well, and the list can be expanded with every new situation, every new occasion for listening more deeply. Bernard Dauenhauer (1980) identifies intimate, liturgical, and malign silences and celebrates the powerful "silence of the to be said." Schools have a more repressed and oppressed range: no mention of the pregnant silence, please, and the hectic competitive pace finds no peace in what Zora Neal Hurston, in a biography without schools, called the "finished silence" (1937/1990). Kathleen Hill's (1999) wonderful recollection of a classroom music teacher plays on a haunting silence for "the anointed." From my own classrooms, whether as student or teacher, I remember being haunted by the twin powers of silence: impending terror and sheer relief.

Schultz transforms the silences of children into opportunities for teachers and students to talk with each other. The struggle of classroom management is not to keep children quiet, nor to get a few of them to contribute at the right time, but to hear and to nurture what is on everyone's mind. The relentless and needless repetition of turn-taking rules and roles that takes up so much teacher time hides a deeper complexity. No one listens to all that noise, and no one, not even teachers, can afford to follow these rules exactly. Teacher controls, social identities, and learning inequalities all seem to be at stake with every passing of a turn to ask or answer. The bigger issue is who gets heard, how, and to what collective ends. Katherine Schultz knows this, and she gives the right advice. We should listen to the silences of the classroom and use her words to help understand them.

Ray McDermott

REFERENCES

Dauenhauer, B. P. (1980). *Silence*. Bloomington: Indiana University Press.

Gross, K. (2001). *Shakespeare's noise*. Chicago: University of Chicago Press.

Hill, K. (1999). The anointed. *DoubleTake, 18*, 83–89.

Hurston, Z. N. (1990). *Their eyes are watching God*. New York: Perennial. (Original work published 1937)

McDermott, R. (2005). In praise of negation. *Zeitschrift für Pädagogik, 50*, 150–70.

Mercier, V. (1977). *Beckett/Beckett*. New York: Oxford University Press.

Yeats, W. B. (1983). "The song of the happy shepherd." In R. Finneran (Ed.), *The poems of W. B. Yeats* (pp. 7–9). New York: Macmillan. (Original poem published 1889)

Acknowledgments

O VER THE YEARS, I have come to realize that I only write in collaboration. At times, it seems that I rarely type a single word that isn't shaped by a conversation or experience with several other people. For a book that has taken many years to write, my debt is large. The order of these acknowledgments is not significant, nor is the list complete. First, I thank two spectacular teachers—Amelia Coleman Brown and Mattie Davis, who, along with their students, graciously invited me into their classrooms over many years. I have continued to learn from Amelia and Mattie and many of their colleagues in two important networks, which have profoundly influenced my thinking—the Philadelphia Writing Project and the Philadelphia Teachers Learning Cooperative. Many individuals have profoundly shaped my thinking on this topic. Rachel Throop helped research and articulate the theoretical frame of the book with incredible insight, intelligence, and precision. Ray McDermott acted as a muse, always willing to talk about silence and sending me a steady stream of wisdom and ideas. Since my first days of graduate school, his writing and thinking have deeply influenced my own. Over many years, several graduate students were engaged in data collection and analysis, writing, and conversations on related projects that under gird much of this book, including Tricia Niesz, Patti Buck, Lalitha Vasudevan, Jennifer Bateman, Carolyn Chernoff, Chonika Coleman, Sharareh Bajracharya, Jennifer Warren, Sally Maxwell, and Rob Connor. In particular, writing with Lalitha Vasudevan and Chonika Coleman has pushed many of these ideas forward, deepening my understanding on many levels. Independent study courses with Rachel Throop, Kristin Searle, and Jennifer Bateman were significant in the development of several of the theoretical notions in the book. Sonia Rosen and Shannon Andrus played important editorial roles in the final stages of the book, helping to fine-tune the prose and offering invaluable advice and insight. Rebecca Steinitz is a stunning editor and dear friend, whose knowledge of writing and education was instrumental in clarifying the ideas in this book. I am enormously grateful for her help and support. Thea Abu-Haj is the ideal writing partner, who brings wisdom and depth to my writing. Conversations with Kathryn Howard before a TESOL conference presentation including her expert transcription have been instrumental in my thinking about silence and participation. Several other colleagues near and far have pushed my thinking forward on topics connected to this book, including Sigal Ben Porath, Bryan Brayboy, Frederick Erickson, Bob Fecho, Rebecca Freeman Field, Joan Goodman, Pam Grossman, Sophie Haroutunian-Gordan, Ann Lieberman, Susan Lytle, Teresa McCarty, Sharon Ravitch, Anna Richert, Ellen Skilton-Sylvester, Doris Warriner, Stanton Wortham, and Nancie Zane and the many members of the listening group. The editors at Teachers College Press, especially Meg Lemke, have provided invaluable advice and insight. Perhaps most importantly, I owe my gratitude to my family, David, Nora, Danny, and Jenna, who teach me, tease me, inspire me and support me in so many ways. Thank you.

Rethinking
Classroom Participation

CHAPTER 1

Participation and Silence in the Classroom

> Speech came out of silence, out of the fullness of silence. The fullness of silence would have exploded if it had not been able to flow out into speech. . . . There is something silent in every word, as an abiding token of the origin of speech. And in every silence there is something of the spoken word, as an abiding token of the power of silence to create speech. (Picard, 1948/1952)

CLASSROOM PARTICIPATION is a ubiquitous idea in education, yet it is rarely defined or elaborated. Classroom participation is understood most often as students' verbal activity; their silence is rarely viewed as a contribution to classroom work and learning. When educators focus on participation, they read certain actions as positive and others as negative. Raising one's hand and providing predictable answers in a whole-class discussion is generally understood to be positive (Cazden 2001; Mehan, 1979). Talking out of turn or to peers, rather than to the whole group, is considered disruptive. When students speak without being called on, teachers often judge whether their participation is positive or negative according to the timing and content of talk and the norms of the classroom. Consider the following example from an urban fifth-grade classroom toward the end of the school year.

> After commanding the students' attention by raising her hand, Amelia Coleman posed the question, "What makes a story good?" As was her custom, she gave the class 4 minutes to write before calling on students. She reminded them to think about what they had learned during the year. After a short period of time, she repeated the question and asked, "Who wants to share first?", calling on the first student who raised his hand. He responded, "Details." Ms. Coleman nodded in agreement and suggested that the other students add this quality of good stories to their own lists. She looked around, calling on students whose hands were raised. She called on a student who was sitting silently. The student stared

1

back at Ms. Coleman without saying a word. Another student filled
in the silence, offering the response, "Themes." Turning toward this
student, Ms. Coleman asked, "What do you mean by themes?" As
other students started to mutter that "themes" was not a good
answer, Ms. Coleman interrupted them saying, "We can help [this
student] really articulate what he means. The underlying message
makes the story good. Who agrees with that?" Most students
nodded. Ms. Coleman linked the idea that a story needs a strong
and clear theme to her framing question. After a brief discussion,
she asked the class to remember a story they had read together
recently and to tell her the theme of that story. Several students
offered responses without raising their hands. Dissatisfied with
their initial answers, she probed until they were able to elaborate
the theme. She connected this skill to what they would need to do
on upcoming tests, explaining, "These are the kinds of questions
they are going to ask you. You have to use everything you know."
The discussion continued as the students added to a chart of the
characteristics of a good story. (field notes, 5/06/05)

In this classroom, as in classrooms throughout the world, students and
teachers enacted prescribed roles. Typically, teachers initiate predictable
routines and, for the most part, students know how and when to respond.
Some teachers follow a guide or script from a teachers' manual, repeating
teaching sequences that match how they learned in school when they were
younger. Others establish alternative patterns of communication through
routines learned at universities and professional development sessions, or
develop their own practices through observation and close listening to their
students. In response, students perform their expected roles, which often
include compliance. In the above scene, Ms. Coleman enacted a sequence
typically found in U.S. classrooms—Initiation Response Evaluation (IRE;
Mehan, 1979)—in which the teacher initiates a question, invites a response, and then evaluates that response or provides feedback.

When Ms. Coleman was met with silence from a single student, she
had to make a quick decision about whether to respond to the silent girl
in the moment, pushing her to give an answer, or maintain the pace of
the lesson for the group. She chose to move on. Rather than insisting that
the girl participate, she allowed another student to offer an answer and
kept the lesson on track. In addition to evaluating the quality of their responses, through a brief series of interactions like this one, the teacher
implicitly—and perhaps unconsciously—evaluated the students as a group
and individually for their participation. Her primary evidence of their participation was whether or not individual students made verbal contribu-

tions to the conversation. A majority of the children in this class participated "successfully" in the lesson through writing or talk, while a scattered few remained silent, their papers blank.

But were these students who were silent simply not participating? Teachers often define classroom participation as a verbal response that fits into a routine or a teacher-established pattern of classroom discourse. Can students participate without speaking out loud? Should educators consider the times that a student gives silent assent to a question or thoughtfully jots notes for a future essay as participation? Are these useful forms of participation? It is important to note that one student's silence can enable another student to speak. Do students have a responsibility to contribute to the silence of a classroom so that others can talk, along with a responsibility to contribute verbally to the discussion? How might silence be reframed as a "productive" or useful contribution to classroom discourse?

Educators tend to have limited understandings of silence in the classroom. Silence is generally viewed as an individual characteristic and educators assume, for instance, that a quiet person is intrinsically shy. Alternatively, teachers assume that silence means a student either does not know the answer or has made an conscious decision not to participate in the discussion. In fact, student silence in the classroom can carry multiple meanings. It can indicate, among other things, resistance, boredom, thoughtfulness, or strategic timing. Silence may manifest simply, but it is a complex phenomenon.

In Ms. Coleman's classroom, the students who spoke aloud to the group were viewed as participants; those who remained silent were not. Ms. Coleman gave students the opportunity to participate through writing as well as talk. As a result, students who remained silent during the discussion but completed their lists and added to them throughout the conversation could be included as participants. In most classes, however, students are only given the opportunity to participate by speaking out loud.

Most often, participation is seen through the lens of talk and, in particular, talk related to topics initiated by the teacher. A singular focus on talk as successful participation obscures the myriad ways that students might also participate through silence. Ms. Coleman appeared to assume that the student who responded with silence when she was called on was a nonparticipant in the classroom discussion. That may have been true. This student may have been distracted or, alternatively, rebellious, refusing to join the classroom community. On the other hand, this student may have taken on a role in this classroom as someone who typically engages through silence. This might be what others, including her teacher, expect of her and what she expects of herself. However, her silence had an important function: It created space for other students to respond.

In this book, I show how silence *can* be a form of participation, and I offer ways for teachers to investigate silence with students. By exploring how students participate through silence, teachers can shift participation structures and revise the linguistic demands of classroom discourse to provide openings for more student engagement. I argue that a student's shyness or reluctance to participate is produced in interaction with teachers and peers, and in response to the classroom environment, the larger social context, and the available roles for students to enact (Wortham, 2006). For instance, a student like the girl who enacted silence in Ms. Coleman's classroom may be shy in one setting, garrulous in another, distracted and rebellious that day, or simply playing her expected role in the group. Understanding a student's silence—or the silence of the group—in relation to the entire system of the classroom allows a teacher to rethink the processes and content of teaching.

Silence is difficult to study and attend to as a teacher and researcher. It is not easy to capture in field notes or through audio and video recorders; indeed, it may completely escape a teacher's or researcher's notice. In order to study silence, I conducted classroom research with graduate students in 10 elementary classrooms over 2 years. As I analyzed the classroom data and explored the research and writing on silence, my focus shifted from silent individuals to the ways silence works in the classroom. I analyzed moments when teachers insisted on silence— on the part of individual students or entire classrooms. I identified the kinds of silences teachers encounter and use in their classrooms and the range of responses to those silences. When teachers express frustration with silent students, they often fail to recognize how silence might be connected more broadly to a larger set of interactions in the classroom that have their own sociopolitical history. As I turned my attention to the interactions, I realized that I needed to look at talk and silence together. Without a measure of silence, there would be no room for talk, and as Picard (1948/1952) explains, the genesis of talk is silence. Ultimately, classroom participation is created in the interactions between talk and silence, both of which become forms of participation.

This book is written for prospective as well as veteran classroom teachers, teacher educators, educational leaders, and educational researchers who seek to understand student and classroom participation and silence more fully. Classroom silence raises questions about participation, expectations, and pedagogical practice. Nearly every educator I speak with— whether at the elementary, secondary, or university level—has a story to tell about silence, from frustration with a student who is so silent it seems impossible to teach her, to the challenge of a class that falls silent when certain subjects, such as race, are broached. Classroom silence raises questions about participation, expectations, and pedagogical practice. Teachers often do not know what to do with silence. It is rarely discussed in teacher education courses or professional development sessions. Through a detailed discussion of the possible meanings of silence, informed by classroom examples of how silence can be used and addressed, this book provides educators and researchers with an array of tools and a broader set of understandings to use in order to understand silence and participation.

I begin in this chapter with an overview of the common meanings of participation and silence in classrooms. Next, I elaborate a sociocultural view of silence, which suggests that silence is located in interactions and contingent on particular contexts and moments in time.

BROADENING NOTIONS OF CLASSROOM PARTICIPATION

There are potentially grave consequences for students when teachers do not understand their silence as a form of participation. Narrow interpretations of the meaning of silence can lead to false assumptions about student participation in classroom activities. For instance, students who are silent might receive low grades for classroom participation, when in fact they are actively engaged in learning. As illustrated later in this book, the particular contributions these students make to the classroom community may be unheard, unrecognized, and discounted. The absence of talk might lead a teacher to assume the absence of learning. It may be difficult for a student to escape the label of the "silent" student. When a teacher does not recognize silence as a form of participation, some students may disengage from school learning and withdraw from the classroom community altogether.

Educators have few metrics for gauging and evaluating participation, especially in classrooms with large numbers of students. Although the term is common, the vocabulary to describe participation is limited. Teacher education programs teach about it, and teachers, administrators, and policymakers seek ways to measure it, but they do so without elaborating its meanings. For example, under the No Child Left Behind Act, the current yardstick for evaluating U.S. schools is Annual Yearly Progress (AYP), which is measured by three scales: performance, participation, and school attendance. But participation is defined simply as showing up to take the test. Individual students often receive participation grades on their report cards. They are generally given high marks if they join in whole-class routines, respond to their teachers in concert with their peers, or offer frequent responses during teacher-led classroom discussions. If they remain silent, following along with the group and only rarely offering their responses, but reflecting deeply on questions and issues, they are often marked with low grades and described as unmotivated, shy, or resistant. In this context, the thoughtful and deliberate student is often judged and described with the same words as the student who, for a variety of reasons, refuses to engage in learning. The silence is attributed to the individual as an internal behavior rather than to the interaction. Some classroom conditions produce silence in some students and talk in others. Furthermore, in order for there to be room for talk, there must be silence; in order for students to be rewarded for their talk, there need to be students who are disadvantaged by their silence (McDermott, 1974; Varenne & McDermott, 1999). Silence can be a sorting mechanism for success and failure.

Although some teachers are flexible about what they consider as participation—for instance, a teacher might count small-group participation, acknowledge written responses, and give students points for preparation—the final participation grade often rests on verbal participation in whole-group discussions. Some teachers have scales in which a quiet or mostly silent student falls near the bottom of the scale, just above the student who refuses to participate or disrupts the class. Grading participation is meant to encourage students to move up the scale, by increasing their verbal participation, which may or may not reflect engagement and thoughtfulness (Bean & Peterson, n.d.).

The challenge of defining and measuring participation is exacerbated by the fact that teachers at all levels, including elementary and secondary school teachers, have few ways to ascertain whether or not a student is learning the school curriculum, and they tend to default to written assessments and measures of verbal contributions to classroom discussions. However, placing this primacy on verbal responses privileges particular students and modes of participation, and often ends up rewarding compliance (e.g., talking because that is what a teacher expects), rather than thoughtfulness and learning. This suggests that in examining whether or not their instructional practices allow for a wide range of student participation, teachers need to consider the nature of their assessment practices, to see if they offer a range of ways for students to participate and show what they know and understand.

Defining Participation

I argue that the first step in defining classroom participation is to understand it as an act that is fundamentally about contribution and connection. In this context, participation consists of any verbal or nonverbal contribution in aural (spoken), visual (pictoral), or written (textual) form that supports learning for the individual student and/or other members of the class. The student who enacts the stance of listening in silence, attending to what is going on and tracking the conversation, might make an important contribution to a classroom discussion by signaling assent to an idea or a willingness to learn from others or through creating a space for another person to speak. If this contribution adds to or extends the understanding of the student or the other participants, the student can be said to participate. Thus, we can define classroom participation as any contribution to a group activity—not just verbal contributions—that creates and extends the spaces for understanding in the classroom.

Recent scholarship provides a useful frame for this understanding of participation. Linguistic anthropologists use the concept of participation to analyze the forms of social organization that are made possible through verbal and nonverbal interactions (e.g., Goffman, 1974, 1981; Goodwin & Goodwin, 2004). For instance, Goodwin (1990) employs this notion to understand how children can strategically use stories to reorganize their social arrangements in the middle of arguments. Disputes between children are usually dyadic, which is to say they involve two people. In her detailed analysis of children's disputes on playgrounds, Goodwin illustrates how children introduce stories to draw outsiders into their arguments to garner support and change the participation framework. She shows that children in the middle of a fight name their peers as actors in the discussion to bolster their position and widen the discussion. As Goodwin and Goodwin (2004) explain, "Participation is intrinsically a situated, multi-party accomplishment" (p. 231). This understanding can be usefully applied to classroom contexts where participation has been generally assumed to be an individual activity.

The concept of a participation framework (Goffman, 1981) is useful in classrooms because it focuses attention on the roles of both speakers *and* hearers in the production of talk and, I would add, silence. According to Goffman, speakers always speak in relation to hearers; their talk is shaped by the social context and the people who are the recipients or targets of their speech. The notion of participation as inclusive of multiple parties and responsive to the social context is important for reframing classroom silence as interactionally produced. Further, Goffman explains that the roles of speaker and hearer are constantly shifting. The term *participation framework* enables the construction of typologies of different kinds of participants or forms of participation in a speech event. This term emphasizes the different rights and obligation of speakers and hearers in various settings. Moreover, Goffman identifies the roles that hearers can take, differentiating, for instance, "ratified" and "unratified" hearers, or the people who are officially part of the conversation and those who are eavesdropping. These concepts are useful for teachers and researchers as they dispel the notion that hearing (or listening) is a passive or static activity; thus, they contribute to a more complex understanding of participation.

More recent work has emphasized the interrelationships between the speaker and hearer, with a focus on the practices actors use to collaboratively co-construct their lifeworlds (Goodwin & Goodwin, 2004), or the contexts they inhabit and act within. Speakers and hearers constantly adjust their words and bodies in relation to one another and their perceptions of the other's relative engagement and disengagement. They do this by raising the pitch of their voices and changing or varying what they say. They respond through their gestures and facial expressions, at times deciding not to speak. This focus on participation as located in situated activities emphasizes the role of the hearer as not simply a passive part of the interaction but an active participant in building the context (Goodwin, 2001). For classroom teachers and researchers, noticing signs of participation in pitch and gesture and seeing these forms of participation in relation to other participants in a particular context opens up greater possibilities for assessing students and understanding their contributions to the classroom discourse.

Addressing Participation in Classroom Practice

Typically, in teacher education classes, prospective elementary and secondary teachers are taught tricks for increasing student participation. Yet these tactics may not provide them with the opportunity to explore and understand silences and students who are silent in their classrooms. In many teacher education classes, prospective teachers are taught to vary their techniques for calling on students in order to increase and control participation. Some days, they might rely on students to volunteer their answers, as Amelia Coleman did in the scene that opened the chapter; on other days, they might call names randomly from note cards or popsicle sticks or use some other technique to ensure that students are prepared and ready to respond at any time. These strategies allow more voices to be heard in a classroom discussion and are meant to hold students accountable. They do not, however, necessarily shift the dynamics of the classroom, nor do they interrogate or address the possible reasons for a student's silence. Further, these techniques focus on increasing the number of students who speak in class; they may not draw in those students who elect to remain silent, nor do they address the conditions that prompt them to participate through silence. Finally, they do not ensure that students respond in ways that increase their learning or the learning of their peers.

Boaler and Humphreys (2005) describe a particularly compelling case from Humphreys's mathematics classroom. They analyze a moment when a teacher's understanding of participation differed from that of her students, leading to a breakdown in the smooth running of the classroom. In response to an article by Hiebert and his colleagues (1997), Humphreys, a high school teacher, became convinced that it was important for all students to participate verbally in class discussions. She was convinced by the assertion made by the authors that "to the extent that some students are excluded and do not participate, the learning possibilities are diminished for everyone" (p. 67). Further, she wondered whether she had failed to hold her students accountable for their learning when she allowed them to remain silent in her class. As an experiment, Humphreys told her students that she would randomly select someone to report on their small-group discussion each day. She hoped this would ensure that everyone would be prepared and comfortable enough to speak aloud.

One day, after a student froze when called on to report for his group, Humphreys turned to the class as a whole to understand this response. The students informed her that they had great difficulty reporting for their classmates. Although Humphreys had thought it would be easier for them to report on a group conversation rather than to volunteer their own responses, they felt that capturing a group conversation was too great a responsibility. Even though Humphreys had repeatedly emphasized the importance of making and learning from mistakes, they were afraid to be wrong about their classmates' understandings. In this case, being wrong meant misrepresenting and potentially disrespecting their classmates, rather than giving the wrong answer to a math problem.

The strategy Humphreys had instituted to increase student participation had not worked because she had inadvertently focused on a certain kind of participation—reporting for others—that was difficult for this group of students. The experience did point out, however, the value of holding a conversation with students about types of participation that both the teacher and students could value and reward. After she went back to a volunteer system for reporting on group discussions, more students began to participate in whole-class discussions. Humphreys concluded that her decision to bring the conversation to the students, prompted by one student's silence, was key to this shift.

Many teachers would not have taken the time (or known how) to engage students in such a conversation. They might have blamed the individual for being shy or not understanding the discussion rather than addressing the broader set of issues that led to his silence. As it turned out, the problem did not rest with the individual at all; instead, it was connected to the rights and obligations for talk and participation that Humphreys had established in her classroom. By trying to distribute the opportunities for verbal participation, she inadvertently introduced a process that constrained talk in the classroom.

Participation carries many meanings and values in a classroom. It is thus wise for a teacher to make these understandings explicit and interrogate what is going on in the classroom when things go awry. Teachers cannot (and should not) assume that they hold the same understandings of participation as their students. As Humphreys's experience illustrates, building an understanding of student perceptions of participation, recognizing how they want to contribute as individuals and group members, and clarifying the teacher expectations may be key to the smooth and productive operation of a classroom.

Recognizing Participation Structures

The concept of participation structures is used by educational researchers to capture the ways teachers organize classrooms to include different kinds of teacher-student and student-student interaction. In research that investigated teacher-student interactions in Warm Springs Indian classrooms, Philips (e.g., 1972) developed the term *participant structure* to highlight the allocation of speaking turns in the variety of classroom organizational structures she observed. Her analysis centered on the mismatch between home and school contexts for learning, which is to say the disparate structures that led to poor school performance for the students. Several other researchers have used this conceptual framework to focus on the notion of participation as tied to school performance and the possibilities for school learning (e.g., Baquedano-Lopez, 2004; McDermott & Godspodinoff, 1979; Mehan, 1979). As Goodwin (2001) explains, "A focus on participation provides the anthropologist an opportunity to study from an integrated perspective how members of discourse communities use language and embodied action to constitute their social worlds" (p. 174).

I use the term *participation structure* throughout this book to refer to the rights and obligations that guide an individual's contributions through talk and silence in classroom interactions. Participation structures are generally introduced and orchestrated by teachers and can explicitly encompass silence, including the teacher's own use of silence in instruction. They include verbal and nonverbal interactions, as well as aural, written, and pictoral contributions. Students can participate through talk and silence, and also through writing or other modes of expression in classrooms where these opportunities exist.

The construct of participation structures provides an analytic framework for studying teacher-student interactions in classrooms, including silence. For instance, Amelia Coleman's decision to hold a whole-class discussion reflected her choice of a particular participation structure, which entailed a set of rights and responsibilities for participation in the event;

on other days, she asked students to talk together in pairs, which was a different participation structure with another set of interactional norms. The idea of participation structures also provides a way to acknowledge and include both verbal and nonverbal contributions to the classroom discourse. Finally, it suggests the need to reframe participation as a collective, rather than an individual, process. Teachers may decide to grade individuals for their verbal contributions to the classroom discourse. However, in doing so, they can neglect the fact that the practice of participation goes beyond the responsibility of a single student and necessarily reflects opportunities created by the teacher and the context of the classroom.

UNDERSTANDING SILENCE AS PARTICIPATION

In recent years, through paying close attention to student talk, educators have refined their tools for understanding what students know and comprehend (e.g., Ball, 1997; Rymes, 2008; Schultz, 2003). In teacher education courses, prospective teachers are taught to focus on students' understandings (or misunderstandings) to gauge student learning. Attention to student talk can ensure that a teacher is focusing in on student learning rather than simply on delivering material. As Ball (1993, 1997) and her colleagues demonstrate, children's verbal explanations can extend a teacher's understandings of students' content knowledge and misconceptions, serving as a guide for pedagogy and curriculum through ongoing formative assessment. I argue here that paying attention to student silence as a form of participation opens up further possibilities for understanding individual students and classroom interactions. It is not easy for teachers to pay attention to what is not said at the same time as they attend to what is said aloud. By articulating the range of meanings of silence and how silence works as a form of participation, I provide teachers and researchers with a set of tools for making sense of a range of types of participation that include silence and, in turn, for broadening their methods of formative assessment.

When teachers invite students to verbally participate in classroom interactions, student silence is most often assumed to indicate disengagement or a failure to participate. Teachers may have few conceptual tools for understanding the students who remain silent in classroom discussions. When faced with this situation, some questions teachers can investigate through careful listening and observation include:

- Were the students who chose not to speak aloud simply shy?
- Did they lack the knowledge or facility with English to participate in the group conversation?

- Were they following cultural practices that guided them to speak only when they had something significant to add to the conversation?
- Did the students who enacted silence act out of conscious resistance, or were they simply daydreaming?

Other questions might require more systematic investigation of the sort I describe in Chapter 5, including:

- Were there local classroom identity politics that determined who had the right to speak at this particular moment in the classroom?
- What was the teacher's role in creating a context that differentially promoted speech and silence?
- What was the role of peers in supporting one another to speak or remain silent?
- How would the discussion have shifted if the teacher had added her own silence?

Without thus investigating the multiple reasons why a student might enact a silent stance, it is difficult to know whether and how she is learning the academic curriculum. Teachers tend to focus on the majority of the students who respond to the classroom routine through predictable verbal contributions, which may leave out the few who remain silent. I suggest that silence has several meanings as it is enacted by students and teachers in classroom interactions and that a nuanced understanding of student silence and talk as participation can shift our conceptions of teaching and learning.

This notion of participation is rooted in the concept of democratic classrooms. Democratic classrooms are often defined as places that highlight access and inclusion, allowing a multiplicity of voices and perspectives to enter into and shape classroom interactions and highlighting the processes of negotiation. In democratic classrooms, teachers and students often negotiate what is learned and how the learning transpires, as well as the sources of knowledge. In democratic classrooms, teachers attend to students' talk and silence (e.g., Dewey, 1944; Roosevelt, 1998a, 1998b; Schultz, 2003). In most classrooms, students' roles and responsibilities for learning are limited, which means that their contributions through silence may be overlooked or may not be well understood by their teachers and peers. Adding a wider range of modes of participation that encourage the negotiation of multiple and varied perspectives expands how we might seek, identify, and enact democratic practices. These practices can be adapted to any classroom, including under resourced classrooms constrained by curricular mandates such as those described in Chapters 3 and 4. As I describe in these chapters, attending to silence, adding silence to classrooms, and shifting participation structures sometimes entails taking only minutes away from academic tasks.

A focus on silence as a form of participation might lead a teacher to create a more democratic classroom that is inclusive of more students and multiple perspectives. Participation is a central component of many conceptions of democratic classrooms. As Maxine Greene (1995) explains:

> Democracy, we realize, means a community that is always in the making. Marked by an emerging solidarity, a sharing of certain beliefs, and a dialogue about others, it must remain open to newcomers, those too long thrust aside. This can happen even in the local spaces of classrooms, particularly when students are encouraged to find their voices and their images. (p. 39)

In order to educate students to participate in democratic processes, it is vital that there are opportunities for all students to participate and more ways for teachers to understand their modes of participation. Central questions for exploring the relationships between participation and inclusive classrooms include:

- What is the nature of this participation?
- Does it always need to be verbal participation, or can we conceptualize a democratic classroom that reflects the perspectives and knowledge of all students without insisting on student talk?
- What are other forms of participation that contribute to democratic and more inclusive practices?
- How does silence figure into this conception of classroom practice?
- What is the teacher's role in understanding and adding silence to a classroom?

I return to these ideas throughout the book and especially in the final chapter.

CONSIDERING PERSPECTIVES ON CLASSROOM SILENCES

In U.S. classrooms, silence generally has a narrow and specific range of interpretations: teachers use silence for positive ends to control their classroom, and alternatively, a student's silence tends to have negative connotations, indicating disengagement. Several different disciplinary interpretations of silence offer educators useful perspectives that can broaden these commonplace meanings. In this book, I argue for a sociocultural conception of silence. Sociocultural theories of learning suggest that learning is

fundamentally a social and cultural activity (rather than an internal or cog-
nitive/behavioral one), which cannot be separated from its historical, cultural, and institutional contexts (e.g., Greeno, 1997; Lave & Wenger, 1991;
Vygotsky, 1978). A sociocultural theory of silence situates the production
of silence in the classroom community demonstrating how it is shaped by
(and in turn shapes) its social and institutional contexts. To elaborate this
understanding of silence, in this section I describe several ways to conceptualize silence that come from a variety of disciplinary perspectives such as
sociolinguistics, literary theory, anthropology, and the arts. Researchers and
theorists conceptualize silence in several overlapping ways which I delin-
eate as a form of communication, as culturally situated and understood, as
chosen rather than imposed, and as spatially and temporally located. Following this discussion, in the next section, I illustrate how these theoretical
understandings can be used to make sense of silence in classroom settings.

Silence as a Form of Communication

Expectations for classroom participation emerge from culturally situated
norms. Across the world, youth are socialized to speak and remain silent
at different times and for different purposes (Saville-Troike, 1985). They
are taught that talk and silence hold different values for communication
between teachers and students, adults and youth. In situations where talk
is highly valued or expected, silence is marked. In other words, if the expectation is that communication occurs through talk, silence and silent
students stand out. In contrast, in his discussion of the use of silence in
the Igbo tribe of Nigeria, Nwoye (1985) explains, "silence in Igbo communication is a figure which reveals its meaning against the ground of speech"
(p. 191). Nwoye suggests that in comparison to the United States, where
talk is paramount, among the Igbo, the locus of communication is silence.
      In U.S. classrooms, as in many classrooms across the globe, there are
implicit and stated rules for talk and silence that are taught to young children when they enter school. For instance, teachers often insist on silence
to signify order and authority in the classroom. Conversely, they also insist on talk, as illustrated by the practice of grading classroom participation according to verbal contributions alone. Teachers' demands for silence
carry the implicit message that students should pay attention. Students
almost always know that when the teacher stands silently at the front of
the classroom, the expected response to her silence is their own silence
and attention. While silence holds multiple meanings for individuals within
and across racial, ethnic, and cultural groups, in American schools, it is
often assigned a limited number of meanings. Students who practice silence are often thought of either as "good" (compliant) or "bad" (resistant

or unintelligent), and their uses of silence are rarely understood as intentional. These norms suggest that talk and silence are fundamentally opposed. However, it is useful to conceptualize silence and talk as interwoven: Silence contains sound and talk always contains silences, suggesting that the binary thinking that often characterizes silence and speech is inadequate (Duncan, 2004).

Within the field of sociolinguistics, silence has been traditionally ignored except for its function of marking boundaries that delimit the beginning and ending of utterances; generally, researchers have defined silence by the absence of speech rather than the presence of silence (Saville-Troike, 1985; Tannen & Saville-Troike, 1985a). The significance of silence is generally measured in relationship to sound, but the opposite is also true: Sound can be understood in contrast to or in relationship to silence. Saville-Troike (1985) writes that it is important to distinguish between silence when no communication occurs and silence that is full of meaning or a part of communication. Silence can be used to organize social relationships, such as silence between people in an elevator. In this case, the silence might have no particular meaning but may signify the act of following an implicit rule (Saville-Troike, 1982). Silence as a form of communication has varied meanings across geographic regions, cultures, and individuals. Too often, its meanings are assumed rather than systematically investigated.

Culturally Situated Understandings of Silence

Community interpretations of silence shape how teachers understand silence in their classrooms. Kiowa writer N. Scott Momaday (1997) describes the meanings of silence in his American Indian community:

> Silence . . . is powerful. It is the dimension in which ordinary and extraordinary events take their proper places. In the Indian world, a word is spoken or a song is sung not against, but within the silence. In the telling of a story, there are silences in which words are anticipated or held on to, heard to echo in the still depths of the imagination. In the oral tradition, silence is the sanctuary of sound. Words are wholly alive in the hold of silence; they are sacred. (p. 16)

In U.S. classrooms, silence has a range of meanings, but it is rarely understood as sacred, the life force of a story and a repository of meaning. Yet, within and across cultures, silence and talk have different values and functions. For instance, the Japanese term *haragei* means "wordless communication" (Saville-Troike, 1982, p. 144). Saville-Troike explains that in the Japanese speech community *haragei* is more highly valued than eloquence. In other words, what people choose *not* to say, or their silence, is more highly valued in some cultures than what they say aloud. Among some speech communities, people believe that as soon as an experience is expressed in words, its real essence disappears. This understanding stands in sharp contrast to expectations in most Western classrooms. The relative silence of some children as compared to others is connected by scholars to childrearing practices and values related to individual achievement, which often reflect cultural norms. When individual achievement is valued, children are thought to talk more. Moreover, children who are brought up with more frequent interactions with adults and older siblings generally do not need to verbalize their needs as much as their peers (Saville-Troike, 1982).

Scollon (1985) suggests that we need to change the metaphors for understanding the meanings of silence, explaining that too often people who are thought to be silent, such as "the silent Indian," are stereotyped as reserved, slow, and detached. Silence is thought to reflect a decision to avoid communication rather than a form of communication on its own (Braithwaite, 1985). In fact, people often choose when, where, and how to communicate through silence, and these decisions often reflect culturally specific patterns of interaction (cf., Braithwaite, 1985; Saville-Troike, 1985; Scollon, 1985). As Cheung (1993) explains, "Silence, too, can speak many tongues, varying from culture to culture" (p. 1). In a wide variety of contexts, there are rules for speech and rules for silence. For example, in his examination of the ways silence is used in 19 communities, Braithwaite (1985) found that silence is often associated with social situations that are ambiguous or uncertain in a variety of ways.

Rather than focusing on the nature of silence, most educational research documents how individuals are silenced (e.g., Fine, 1987, 1991; Schultz, 2003) and perspectives that are omitted from a curriculum (e.g., Delpit, 1995). Silencing is often conceptualized as the act of disempowering students through prescribed norms, texts, and interactions. Silencing acts and structures enforce silence in certain individuals. As a result, students who enact silence are usually considered to be disadvantaged by their silence. For instance girls, students of color, LGBTQ (lesbian, gay, bisexual, transgender, queer/questioning) students, and students with special needs are often assumed to be silenced rather than silent by choice or silent by circumstance. However, by narrowing our focus to the ways in which teachers, peers, and schools as institutions silence certain students—that is, by coding silence as always negative—we miss the opportunity to explore how silence itself is too often silenced (Li, 2004; Schultz, 2008). In other words, a negative reading of silence obscures the useful and educational aspects of silence detailed later in this book.

Silence as a Choice

Although students can be silenced, they also choose silence. Students strategically use silence to protect themselves, to buy time, as a form of expression, and as a way to participate in a conversation. In classrooms, teachers insist on silence (to draw attention to their talk) or they insist on talk (to display learning). Their goal is often to give "voice" to silent students, to coax them into talk, rather than to understand the meanings of their silence.

For a teacher, silence might signal that a student is following directions and engaged in individual work or it might indicate student disinterest, boredom, and even hostility. Silence is often thought to indicate shyness, powerlessness, and fear, but rarely is it understood as the choice not to speak. When it is understood as a refusal to speak, silence is assumed to be a passive expression of opposition or hostility, rather than an act of agency that could even be participatory. A teacher might interpret a student's silence as lack of preparation or knowledge, or even as ignorance, and that interpretation can become the basis of a label that is attached firmly to the student. As Gal (1991) explains, schools judge, sort, define, and categorize on the basis of talk. I would add that they also make these decisions based on silence. In these instances, a student can be said to be silenced. But we can also examine how a student actively takes on silence in response to particular context and circumstances.

Spatial and Temporal Locations of Silence

> We had to conceive of silence in order to open our ears. (Cage, 1973)

Rather than defining silence as a void, a silent response as empty, and a silent student as passive, we can understand silence as a container of meaning. The composer John Cage illustrates this in his composition "4'33"," which is 4½ minutes of silence. Cage explains that music is continuous while silence occurs when we turn away, elaborating that his work is "an exploration of nonattention" (Cage, 1961, p. 22). Through this musical piece in which the musicians and conductor remain still without emitting a sound for over 4 minutes, Cage forces the audience to attend to the silence, as it fills with sounds and meanings rather than the music they expect. In this book, drawing on this concept, I invite teachers and researchers to consider student and classroom silences as openings into repositories of meaning.

In a typical classroom, students spend a large portion of their time sitting in silence. Silence occurs when there are pauses; there is silence when space is left around words and phrases. Scholars suggest that art, music, writing, language, and other forms of creativity arise out of silence. In this sense, silence is not a void but rather a populated—and at times protected—location that fosters creativity and thought. When a student stares off into space, her teacher might assume that she is distracted and her mind empty. That may be the truth. It also may be that the student is working something out that is directly related to the conversation at hand; her silence allows her time to think more deeply about a question or topic.

Silence can also be woven into writing: in both its production and consumption. We often read and write in silence, and we add silence to our writing and also to our reading. Pauses in writing are indicated by spacing and punctuation. Japanese literature has a silence marker (Saville-Troike, 1985). In music, silences are marked by rests. A *caesura* marks the transition from one musical phrase to another. In classrooms, as in the world at large, meaning transpires out of silence.

Silence also inhabits physical spaces. For example, Constable (2005) explains that when we enter libraries, we imagine a sign that commands "silence," although these signs rarely exist. We have learned that the library space signifies silence, and we act accordingly, speaking softly. The space of the Quaker meetinghouse signals silence when participants enter for individual and communal reflection. These spaces of and for silence remind us that silence makes some activities and practices possible. For instance, silence in these spaces can be used to center and quiet the mind. It can also be used to formulate plans of action and determine next steps for individuals and the collective group. In classrooms, such as the one described in Chapter 3, silence can allow a student to hold onto his authorial voice. There are necessary silences, and at times, these silences are connected to specific places and times. We often pause to honor the death of a person, using the silence to signify respect and attention. That silence is often considered necessary and generally understood without explanation. Other times and locations may signal silence to some but not all participants. A particular class activity, such as a literature discussion, may draw some students immediately into the talk and others into their own silence.

Rather than focusing on the definitions of silence, scholars such as Zembylas and Michaelides (2004) urge educators to pay attention to how silence works in a classroom:

> Seeking to nurture, to educate, to inspire, silence in educational settings may reach places that speech can, at best, only evoke. The difficulty is first to identify and call attention to the various kinds of silence in the public context of the classroom and then to create spaces that nurture, challenge or enrich these silences. (p. 203)

Rather than eliminating silence, the authors urge educators to create opportunities for silence in classrooms, paying attention to its functions and meanings (see also Burbules, 2004; Li, 2004; Schultz, 2003).

A focus on silence as participation suggests attending to the limitations of talk rather than ascribing limitations to the silent individual (Schultz, 2008). As Cage and others illustrate, there are ideas that can be conveyed far more effectively and powerfully through silence rather than through sound. Further, silence is often collectively produced and individually assigned. It is easier to locate silence as an internal characteristic of a person rather than a strategy for expressing particular ideas. Wittengenstein (1961) warns, "There is indeed the inexpressible. . . . Whereof one cannot speak, thereof one must be silent" (p. 149). Zembylas and Michaelides (2004) add, "There is a futility in making everything into another content of speech; some things are lost in the speaking. It might be argued that this loss is silence itself" (pp. 194–195). Silence can be understood as a container for ideas that cannot be expressed in words. Further, silence is often, although not always, filled with meaning and possibilities.

APPLYING SOCIOCULTURAL THEORIES OF SILENCE TO CLASSROOM SETTINGS

Every utterance has its biography and cuts its own figure, and, if we are careful enough to describe its points of contact with ongoing events, we can learn a great deal about the powers of talk that constructs, maintains, and resists the order of those events. (McDermott, 1988, p. 38)

In place of the commonly held notion that certain students are intrinsically silent, silence in classrooms can be usefully understood as a product of interactions located in a particular time and location. Like all utterances, silence has a biography that reflects its history and current context, including the people and patterns of interaction that surround it. Bakhtin (1981) offered a view of language as inherently social and always undergoing transformation. According to Bakhtin, our language—and, I would argue, our silence—becomes our own only after we have appropriated it from others. In other words, our silence and talk are not our own; they are socially produced in interaction with others.

In classrooms, silence occurs through interactions between and among students and teachers in response to widely circulating and locally produced discourses, or ways of speaking and acting that reflect certain beliefs and identities (Gee, 1996; Wortham, 2006). Individuals are more likely to be quiet in only some situations than intrinsically silent. Rather than focusing on silent individuals, I suggest that educators focus attention on how silence and vocal participation are constructed through interaction between and among students and teachers in response to particular circumstances and contexts, shaped by larger societal patterns or discourses. The interactional ways in which silence is produced are reflected in the following vignette drawn from a seventh- and eighth-grade Cherokee classroom.

> Mr. Miller's classroom is one of the most difficult to be in, for even if it is quiet—at times a long breath has a piercing quality—that silence tells more than any number of words can. It is threatening, frustrating, condemning, rage-filled, and it expresses understanding, compliance, acquiescence, and defeat. The slightest motions, a change in posture or a facial expression, are cause for immediate attention, for they mean a shift in the meaning of silence. Every different form that it takes is also a different kind of tension, which is never absent but only varies in intensity depending upon what Mr. Miller does. (Dumont, 1972, p. 355)

In the above passage, researchers describe their experience in this Cherokee classroom taught by a White teacher. Dumont describes the silence as located in the relationships among the participants. When Dumont and his colleagues first observed Cherokee classrooms, they concluded that the silence indicated that the students did not know how to respond to the teacher's questions, determining that the silence was a behavior or characteristic of individual students. They postulated that the silence was a reflection of language differences, the students' shyness, or a characteristic particular to this group of American Indians. After observing in the classrooms over time, however, Dumont learned how the teacher and his students interactionally produced silence. Silence, he concluded, was the nerve center through which learning transpired. As he explained:

> What is behind the words and the silence, illusory and perceived only part of the time by the teacher and student and the effects intensely felt by both but never verbalized, governs the course of education. In this incident, which is but one of many, no one wins: teacher and student are pulled farther apart, and the strategies of preaching and silence are refined and made even more destructive. (p. 357)

Through rich description of the classroom, Dumont elaborates the downward spiral that began with a misinterpretation of silence and ended with heightened emotions and misunderstanding.

In an earlier study located in Ogala Sioux classrooms where there were similar patterns of silence, the same researchers observed teacher professional development meetings to learn more about the teachers' understandings of the student silence. In both locations, the (White) teachers described the students as shy, withdrawn, indifferent, fearful, and unwilling to compete with each other. Initially, the teachers were told to respond to these behaviors by encouraging the students to "talk up." As a result, the teachers cajoled, commanded, and often shouted at their students to speak. Despite this great effort, there continued to be long periods of silence in the classrooms. When students spoke, their responses were often barely audible. In contrast, researchers observed that outside of classrooms students were noisy, boisterous, daring, and curious. When they wanted to learn something, the students were not shy or withdrawn, and there were few language difficulties.

Dumont concluded that the Ogala Sioux and Cherokee students used silence to control classroom discourse in order to exclude their teacher. When the research team returned the following summer, they sought to discover whether the silence could be broken. They learned that the students were talkative when the teaching and learning was located in the community. Once back in their classrooms, the students resumed their silent stance. It became clear that the students were not silent people—as American Indians have often been described—instead, they produced silence in their interactions with teachers, especially when these interactions were located in the context of school.

Locating his initial work in Ivy League universities, Brayboy (e.g., 2004) describes how American Indian students choose strategies that make them both visible and invisible depending on the context. He relates an event when an American Indian undergraduate decided not to correct the misinformation her professor gave to the class about her own tribe. She privileged her understanding garnered from her cultural background and her cultural integrity, what Brayboy terms her "Indianess," choosing to remain silent and invisible rather than verbally participating in the class. Her silence was thoughtfully chosen and situationally specific. Her "Indianess" was not shyness but rather action based on deference and respect enacted in the moment.

Research on silence and participation in American Indian communities highlights the importance of locating an understanding of silence in the interactions among specific people in particular contexts and time periods. As McDermott (1988) suggests in his essay on inarticulateness, a sociocultural account of silence asks us to examine the conditions under which people are silent and the conditions that lead them to become talkative. He explains, "Occasions in which people are left without words are systematic outcomes of a set of relations among a group of persons bound in a social structure" (p. 38). In other words, institutions, interactions, and power dynamics create conditions for silence. Inarticulateness is a good example of this phenomenon. The conditions that make some people seem articulate and others inarticulate are rarely examined, even though the most articulate among us can remember moments when they were rendered speechless.

There are several groups of people who are commonly stereotyped as silent in U.S. schools, including American Indians, Asian students, disaffected students (who may or may not be students of color), and timid, middle-class, adolescent White girls. Portraits of "silent Indians" or "shy Asian Americans" locate the silence in the individuals rather than the interactions and social context. Examining the literature on silent groups of students through a sociocultural lens provides an important way to understand how silence works in classrooms and can lead to an understanding of the meanings and functions of student silence across contexts.

For example, Asian girls are often praised for their silence, which is often equated with compliance. As Cheung (1993) explains:

> The quiet Asians are seen either as devious, timid, shrewd, and, above all, "inscrutable"—in much the same way that women are thought to be mysterious and unknowable—or as docile, submissive, and obedient, worthy of the label "model minority," just as silent women have traditionally been extolled. (p. 22)

According to Cheung, there are dichotomous ways of describing Asian women. However, Lee (2005) complicates this stereotype in her study of Hmong American students in a U.S. high school. There, students were identified as "good" when they participated in school activities, including lively classroom discussions. Lee explains that the two Hmong American students in the classroom she observed were generally quiet, likely because they lacked the fluency and knowledge of rules for participation that reflected the White, middle-class norms of the school.

Writing about a similar phenomenon in her fictional memoir *Woman Warrior*, Maxine Hong Kingston (1989) explains:

> It was when I found out I had to talk that school became a misery, that the silence became a misery. I did not speak and felt bad each time that I did not speak. I read aloud in first grade, though, and heard the barest whisper with little squeaks come out of my throat. "Louder," said the teacher, who scared the voice away again. The other Chinese girls did not talk either, so I knew the silence had to do with being a Chinese girl. (p. 166)

In this instance, a young girl's silence was read by her teachers, her classmates, and herself as an ethnic characteristic she brought into the classroom. She—along with her teacher and peers—did not understand the ways that society was organized to create her as a silent student and how she and her peers colluded in this form of labeling. The social organization of school and the narrow definitions of participation located the silence as an internal characteristic, identifying her as a silent Chinese girl. It is likely that her teachers assumed and accepted her silence rather than shifting the participation structures in the classroom to encourage her talk. At times, she may have enjoyed this label, while at other times, it was likely perceived as a deficit that defined and limited her engagement in school. Viewed from a sociocultural perspective, this silence can best be understood through the examination of the situated context in which she performed silence and was perceived by others to be a silent student. The silence was not "her" silence but a silence constructed and maintained by everyone in the classroom, reinforced by socially agreed upon stereotypes.

Drawing on long-term research in an American Indian community, Basso (1990) writes about how individual Western Apache Indians' decisions to speak or remain silent depend on social relationships. He discovered that in this community a person's silence often indicates that social relations are ambiguous, unpredictable, or threatening. For instance, meeting strangers or people separated by social distance requires an initial silence. For members of this community, it is important to be in another's company for a period of time before speaking. Outside introductions are viewed as presumptuous and unnecessary. This is related to the belief that forming social relationships is serious and takes time, caution, and careful judgment. Such beliefs and behaviors can play a significant role in shaping decisions to remain silent in the classroom, as in the world outside of the classroom.

In the late 1960s, anthropological and sociolinguistic research offered primarily group-based explanations for students' silence in school (e.g., Gilmore, 1985; Philips, 1983; Tannen & Saville-Troike, 1985b). This research problematized the silence of marginalized groups of students in classrooms and highlighted teachers' roles in this silencing. The result was a focus on creating inclusive participation structures that provided opportunities for talk and interaction (e.g., Au & Mason, 1981; Erickson & Mohatt, 1982; Philips, 1983). Often, these participation structures were designed with certain groups in mind so that classrooms became more culturally responsive. The intent was to establish classrooms that were respectful, building on student strengths rather than remediating the perceived deficits that students brought from their home communities. Frequently, the goal was to increase talk in order to increase student participation. The implication was that the talk is a proxy for learning and that different groups talk or remain silent in different ways.

This research, focused on groups of students susceptible to failure in school, often grew out of explanations of cultural mismatch; certain students did poorly in school because their home cultures did not match the school traditions and expectations. These kinds of conclusions were based on the assumption that students come from unified cultures and that a single culture—often, a middle-class White culture—is enacted in the classroom. More recent sociocultural and linguistic anthropological theories offer explanations of how individual and group norms are always constructed in the moment and in relationship to larger sociocultural patterns of interaction. For instance, Wortham (2006) offers an explanation for social identification based on the theory that individuals draw on models of identity that are locally produced and, at the same time, widely circulating across time and space. Holland, Lachicotte, Skinner, and Cain (1998) describe what they call "identity in practice" (p. 271) and explore its relationship with agency. According to Holland and her colleagues, people construct their identities within contexts of "figured worlds" or culturally shared practices. The authors highlight the importance of improvisation as a practice that describes "where—along the margins and interstices of collective cultural and social constructions—how, and with what difficulties human actors, individuals, and groups are able to redirect themselves" (p. 278) or act with agency. According to these theories, people take on identities in relation to context and experience. The identities are not intrinsic or separate from social contexts and interactions; rather, they are embodied and enacted in practice. Thus, the silence of the Chinese girls described by Hong Kingston or the Cherokee students in Dumont's studies can only be understood by looking at the total constellation of interactions in their classrooms at a particular moment. A teacher can make sense of their identities as "silent students" by looking at how silence is produced in local classroom settings that change over time. The students are not always silent; they are silent in response to locally specific contexts and activities. Further, as Wortham (2006) explains, students work together to construct their peers as certain kinds of people, including silent ones.

Understanding how silence works and investigating this silence with students, as I describe in Chapter 5, can lead to a greater understanding of the possibilities for teaching and learning. The purpose of this survey of some of the meanings of silence has been to elaborate commonplace understandings and build a sociocultural framework for understanding silence in the classroom. Framing silence as a mode of interaction and a form of participation that reflects local contexts and specific moments in time shifts conventional understandings and assumptions about "silent" students locating the explanation in the broader context of the classroom setting. This suggests a different approach and set of strategies for responding to silence elaborated in subsequent chapters.

PLAN OF THE BOOK

In this book, I suggest ways to understand a student's silence or the silence of the group as related to the entire system of the classroom and as a product of larger sociocultural patterns. In addition, I describe how teachers might deliberately use silence in their classrooms. Chapter 2 explores the ways students enact silence as I elaborate how silence functions in the classroom and the forms it might take. I elucidate five ways students use silence to perform different functions in classrooms as representative of the range of meanings of silence. Silence can be a form of resistance; a student may refuse to comply with a teacher's request or a school policy out of defiance or for a variety of other reasons, such as a reluctance to perform in public. Students use silence to assert power. Alternatively, students enact a silent stance as protection. Students are often silent in response to trauma. Finally, students can use silence as a space in which to build their imaginations or to solidify knowledge. This chapter draws attention to this range of ways that students enact silence in order to open up new possibilities for teachers and researchers to understand and respond to student silences.

In Chapter 3, drawing on patterns of interaction in a first-grade classroom, I explore the rules for classroom participation and the ways various participation structures allow for and are shaped by different kinds and amounts of talk and silence. I begin with a discussion of how silence can be integral to a teacher's pedagogical practices and student learning. Then I explore the ways that a teacher, Mattie Davis, introduces silence or silent periods of time into her classroom, as well as how she breaks silence through the creation of new structures that increase or shift student participation.

Chapter 4 explores ways to rethink curriculum to address—without eliminating or replacing—student silence and to provide students with alternate ways to participate in classrooms where silence may not be acceptable. I show how Amelia Coleman, the fifth-grade teacher introduced at the beginning of this chapter, worked with a team of researchers to construct a curriculum that reflected the lives, experiences, and cultural understandings of the children in her classroom. Adding multimodalities to a classroom is one way that a teacher can increase active participation and allow students to have what I call a participatory presence in the classroom. This is not to suggest that teachers should always seek to eliminate silence from their classrooms. I suggest instead that teachers learn to read student silences for clues about how to provide more possibilities for student participation.

Finally, in Chapter 5, I describe how teachers might take an inquiry stance toward the silence in their classrooms in order to understand the multiple meanings and possibilities for silence in their teaching. This chapter provides specific tools to investigate talk and silence in classrooms. In addition, the chapter explores implications for teacher education, emphasizing how important it is for new and prospective teachers to practice noticing student silence in order to understand student talk.

Teachers may yearn for silent classes. When a class is out of control or simply too noisy, a teacher may seek the quiet silence brings. Conversely, teachers might dread silent classes. When the teacher asks a question and no one ventures an answer, teaching may come to a halt, leading the teacher to craft a new plan. At times, the solution is to rephrase the question. In other instances, the teacher may need to change the topic and approach it from a new direction. Sometimes she might simply give the responsibility for the discussion over to the students. In any case, silence often causes teachers to rethink their teaching. Every teacher has encountered uncomfortably silent classrooms and students who enact silence. There may be students who rarely speak or only speak in certain circumstances. It is often difficult for a teacher to gauge how much a student who may refrain from speaking aloud is learning. Sometimes students who are silent can be convinced to speak; other times, they hold tightly to their silence.

This book examines silent students and silent classrooms in order to broaden and deepen teachers' and researchers' understandings of this phenomenon and to reframe it as a contribution or "silent voice." Rather than eliminating the presence of silence and negating students who enact silence in classrooms, the goal is to illuminate and provide tools for understanding the multiple forms and functions of silence, its role in teaching and learning, and the ways it might be understood as a form of participation.

CHAPTER 2

Forms and Functions of Silence

A closeted gay student sat in the back of her high school English classroom. She loved this class, especially its focus on writing. She thought of herself as a poet and kept a daily journal. However, she had decided to refrain from talking in this class to protect herself from her classmates' bigotry. She wrote poems about her life and her choices that did not seem to resonate with her peers, and as a result, she chose silence, even as she followed the discussion, seeking ways to contribute without drawing attention to herself. (adapted from Blackburn, 2002/2003)

NOISY STUDENTS and classrooms tend to cause teachers greater concern than silent ones. While teachers may feel the need to control or manage raucous students, silent students tend to play into a teacher's understandable desire for order and for the most part, they may seem easier to teach. In order to distinguish between individual students in their classrooms, teachers often ascribe labels to students who stand out because of either their loudness or their silence. These may be unspoken labels that act as a filter through which the teacher perceives and understands the students' actions. Alternatively, they may be labels developed unconsciously by the class as a whole. Labels such as "silent student" might be affixed to individuals, while other labels assign silent traits to groups, sorted by categories such as gender, race, class, and sexuality. "Painfully shy" is an example of an individual label; quiet Asian students, loud Black girls, and silent American Indians are examples of group categories.

Yet these labels are inevitably inadequate. Teachers may attribute a student's shyness to his personality or home situation without considering why the student is shy in the specific context, what acting shy means to him, and how he has been constructed by others—and himself—as shy. For instance, if a teacher does not know that a student is gay and is unaware of the teasing that occurs outside of the classroom, the teacher may not know how to read the student's silence, which is likely the product of several intersecting factors. For students who fit into groups conventionally viewed as silent, teachers may assume, without enough information, that their silence has specific connotations such as compliance, insecurity, resistance, or boredom, even though, as illustrated in Chapter 1, the meanings of silence are far more varied and particular. Jensen (1973) explains that "Silence can communicate scorn, hostility, coldness, defiance, sternness, and hate; but it can also communicate respect, kindness, and acceptance" (p. 252). Often, more than one descriptor is needed to capture the qualities or behaviors of individuals and groups: An individual's silence might reflect hostility in one moment and respect in another.

It is all too easy to read silence through a group lens. As we saw in Chapter 1, educators may assume that Asian American students are quiet and compliant as a group and that American Indian students are reticent in certain kinds of discussions. These characterizations can be a useful device, especially when a teacher has a large class filled with many students. However, they usually collapse when the silence is examined as a phenomenon that is socially produced and contextually specific. For the most part, variation within a group is comparable to or greater than variation across groups. Recognizing group patterns helps educators to make adaptations in their classroom structures and routines. Seeing individual variation within those patterns allows teachers to know their students as individuals and support their particular strengths and vulnerabilities (Pollock, 2004, 2008; Schultz, 2008). Understanding how these patterns vary according to the local context and social milieu gives teachers a greater understanding of the classroom dynamics as well as how silence and students who enact silence shape and are shaped by circulating models of how to be a student (Wortham, 2006).

As an introduction to the central concepts of this chapter, I begin with a brief description of a high school student, Luis, whose story I elaborate later in the chapter.

> Luis was a poet who grew up in a Mexican American family that had deep roots in a local gang. He spoke Spanish to his parents at home and English at school. After he witnessed the shooting and subsequent death of a close friend, he made the decision to leave his gang and apply himself in school. He asked for and was given permission to leave the gang. The subsequent shift in his attitude in school was barely perceptible to his teachers. He still chose a seat in the back of the room and rarely spoke. While he was usually attentive to the conversations and completed his assignments, he carried himself in a way that conveyed disengagement, cloaking his deep interest in a range of subjects. All the same, his classmates and teachers knew to listen carefully when he did speak, as his contributions often contained insight that shifted the tenor or direction of a conversation.

Although it is tempting to try to identify a single source for Luis's silence, in fact several overlapping ways of understanding silence provide a more nuanced picture of the role of silence in Luis's interactions with his peers, his teacher, and the local context of the classroom. Luis's teachers generally concluded that he was a resistant student. Yet, as I argue in this chapter, what sometimes looks like resistance can also be understood as a strategy Luis used to enact his own beliefs about what participation should look like in school. Simply put, he participated when he deemed it important and remained silent when he felt that he had nothing to add. By choosing when to speak, he frequently made contributions that were consequential for the class discussion: His words and his silence were powerful. The silence that preceded and followed his talk often highlighted what he said, attracting his classmates' and teachers' attention.

Luis's silence extended from the classroom to his own life: He chose what to reveal about his home life and interests and when to shroud those topics in silence, keeping them separate from school. For instance, he rarely revealed his notebook of poetry, appearing to guard its contents as if to protect them—and, by extension, himself—from a threatening world. Like most students in high-poverty urban schools, Luis's decision to remain in school was closely connected to trauma, as were his silences. Although they were present in his poetry, these traumatic events were not easily captured in words spoken aloud. Finally, Luis used silence outside of school and also within the school day to reflect and gather his thoughts. The time he needed may have been related to his status as an English Language Learner or it may have been more closely connected to his desire to write poetry as a means of expression. Although he may have appeared at times to be distracted, he was often working on composing a poem or puzzling over a statement he heard or read in class. At these moments, his silence belied his attention and engagement in school.

In this chapter, I explore the five categories of silence manifest in Luis's experience: silence as resistance, silence as power, silence as protection, silence as a response to trauma, and silence as a space for creativity and learning. The categories come from my own classroom research, which involved systematic observation and documentation, as well as published research reports and literature on silence from a range of disciplines. As in the case of Luis, although I discuss the categories separately, the functions and uses of silence are multifaceted and often appear together. The categories are meant to be suggestive rather than definitive, to prompt new ways to conceptualize the forms and functions of silence in classrooms and, perhaps more important, to give teachers, students, and researchers new ways to understand student silence and how silence works in classrooms.

SILENCE AS RESISTANCE

One of the more common explanations for silence is that it represents a student's resistance to learning or participating in a classroom activity. This generally has a negative connotation. However, there are many possible ways to understand silence as resistance. Silence might reflect a refusal to learn or to engage in the teacher's lesson for a set of complex reasons (e.g., Kohl, 1994; Schultz, 2002). Reframing resistance as nuanced and contextual rather than simply negative suggests a broader understanding of silence and resistance as forms of participation. Through silence, a student can simultaneously resist an assignment and participate in the classroom, as illustrated in the following vignette drawn from an ethnographic study of students' transitions from high school to the workplace (Schultz, 2002, 2003).

> Denise was poised to graduate from high school. She had passed all of her courses and the state exams in reading and mathematics. All that remained for her to complete was a senior project. Earlier in the year she had led a student protest against the senior project, claiming that the students were not told about it early enough in the year and that the teachers had changed the rules, enacting one more barrier to graduation. Despite the protests, the senior project remained a requirement, with some modifications. When her English and government teachers informed Denise that she was required do the senior project, which included a public presentation to a community panel, she responded with silence. She simply refused to engage in a conversation about the project, and specifically about the public performance. Holding her ground, she refused to speak whenever they broached the topic. For days there was a standoff. In the end, the teachers broke the silence by offering a compromise. Denise was given the option of making an audiotape of her presentation for a panel of evaluators to listen to outside of school, eliminating the public component of the project. Denise complied and graduated. (adapted from Schultz, 2003)

In this instance, the student's silence represented a refusal to comply with a required classroom or school activity. This was not Denise's first act of resistance. Although a good student, Denise often simply refused to do an assignment. She would sit in silence at the back of the room until the class had finished the assignment and then re-engage with the class. These assignments were nearly always group projects that included some kind of presentation. She did not like to work collaboratively with her peers and, in particular, she disliked standing in front of the class. Denise was also stubborn. In her view, the teacher should impart information; her role was to passively receive that knowledge and display it on individual tests and papers. If the teacher did not enact her role, Denise refused to comply with the directions. She was a strong enough student that these moments of refusal—and silence—did not significantly affect her grades.

The senior project was a different story because Denise's refusal to participate jeopardized her chances for graduation. Her teachers did not allow this silent refusal to go unanswered and engaged her in a compromise. The stakes were simply too high. Denise explained in interviews that she resisted the senior project because she was shy about speaking in front of people and unwilling to be part of a public performance. Her resistance to the senior project and other class projects had nothing to do with her disconnection from school, nor was it a political statement. In fact, Denise was present and engaged in most school activities. Student resistance, and the silence that is a manifestation of resistance, can take several forms, including those that Denise displayed. Often, students resist out of a lack of interest in the content of their learning or because they do not recognize a compelling reason to be in school or do the teacher's assignments. Their silence might reflect their—sometimes accurate—assessment of their poor chances of succeeding through active participation in school. This resistance may take the form of silence, or it might be reflected in the choice to sit in the back of the classroom talking to peers, through the instigation of loud angry debates, or any number of other stances. It is not singularly conceived.

There are other reasons for students to enact silence as a resistant stance. Choosing not to speak can be an act of refusal to be dominated (Duncan, 2004). As Minh-ha (1990) explains, like speech, silence operates as a discourse and as a will to "unsay" or refusal to participate in dominant discourses. A refusal to participate opens up possibilities for telling new stories. Denise's decision not to perform her senior project in public led her to craft a tape that represented her ideas in a thoughtful, nuanced manner. A student may resist verbal participation because the possibilities for speech or contributions to a discussion appear too limiting. If only certain discourses are allowed, it may not be worth speaking. Students make these kinds of decisions individually and collectively. Teachers can blame silent, resistant individuals or classes, labeling them as lazy, or they can rethink the form and content of their own teaching and the expressive opportunities they offer students. As I illustrate in Chapter 4, although they are often constrained by curricular mandates and the pressures of testing, teachers can attend to the interests of their students and their preferred formats for learning to shift their pedagogical practices.

Fordham (1996) explains resistance as the willful refusal to learn. She claims that this stance differs from the failure to learn and also from conformity, which she defines as the "unqualified acceptance of ideological claims of society" (p. 39). Resistance, according to Fordham, can also indicate a student's desire to achieve in school, disproving low expectations held by others. Fordham (1993, 1996) claims that the conformity and subsequent achievement of high-achieving Black females, earned through silence, enabled them to resist the low expectations held for them by their teachers and school administrator, ultimately leading to their academic success.

It is critical, however, for teachers to learn how to understand and address student resistance, rather than allowing students to refuse to participate in class simply because the teacher understands the reasons behind their resistant stance. Resistance through silence often appears to be a lack of involvement in learning. In Capital High School, Fordham (1996) explains that students' silence and resistance belied their active engagement in learning and school success. More often, however, resistance linked to silence appears to be passive. When teachers encounter passive resistance, out of frustration they frequently blame the student rather than looking closely at the larger educational context and their pedagogical and curricular choices. It is difficult to know what to do with a persistently silent and resistant student.

If resistance is understood as intrinsic to the individual (e.g., the student is an angry, bored, or disinterested person), there are relatively few interventions for a teacher to initiate. On the other hand, if resistance is reframed as collaboratively organized, there are several approaches a teacher might take to reorganize the classroom into a democratic space that recognizes and respects students, such as those classrooms described in Chapter 3 and 4. Making room for a range of perspectives and ways to engage students in learning may lead students to become more involved in learning through their silences. Rather than seeking to eliminate silence or resistance, teachers can use tools to analyze the classroom participation structures, assignments, and assumptions about their students to rethink the available avenues for engagement, as I describe in Chapter 5. Neither silence nor resistance is an individual act chosen by a student. Rather, they are collaborative activities constructed in relationship to a complex set of classroom and larger societal dynamics.

Writing about women, and particularly Black women, Lorde (1984) reminds us, "We need to hear both the voices and silences through which women engage the social world. We need to understand not only what women say but also what they refuse to say and understand why they might refuse to speak" (p. 42). This desire to recognize both voice and silence can extend to all participants in classrooms. Rather than eliminating silence, Lorde proposes the need to understand why someone might refuse to speak and what she might refuse to say. This analysis suggests that silence in the form of resistance, or the refusal to participate in classroom learning, should not simply be understood as a negative stance toward learning and participation. It can also be understood as a logical response to a complex, politically charged situation.

SILENCE AS POWER

There is a silence that cannot speak. There is a silence that will not speak. (Joy Kogawa, 1982)

As the case of Denise illustrates, acts of resistance are often closely connected to uses of power. The following scene, drawn from a longitudinal study of the literacy practices of high school students in a multiracial high school on the West Coast (Schultz, 2003), highlights Luis, the student introduced at the beginning of the chapter, and illustrates how he used silence to enact a powerful stance in his classroom. This single moment was a product of several other such moments that, over time, represented an individual pattern or characteristic use of silence and talk for this student in this classroom.

> Luis sat in the back row of his high school government class. The topic of discussion was the historical role of J. Edgar Hoover as director of the FBI, a topic they had been talking about for weeks. Students spoke passionately about their views of Hoover and his role in building the FBI. As they vied for the floor, students' voices spilled over one another. His notebook open, Luis had remained silent for weeks on end. It was not until close to the end of the first semester that he uttered his first statement to the whole group. When he spoke, Luis delivered a powerful indictment of the growing consensus in the class, reminding everyone, including the teacher, of the film they had recently viewed which revealed Hoover's anti-gay stance. In a rare moment of silence, his classmates listened carefully to his words. His statement changed the course of the conversation, which resumed with renewed energy and emotion when he finished speaking.

Initially, both his teacher and I had interpreted his stance—slumped deep into his seat in the back of the room, wearing clothing generally labeled by teachers as "gang-related," and looking bored—to mean that Luis was disengaged from school. Occasionally, we wondered if he lacked the knowledge to participate in the rapid-fire discussions that characterized this multiracial, yet predominantly African American, classroom. I speculated that his relative lack of facility with English contributed to his infrequent participation in classroom discussions. At first, neither his teacher nor I asked him to explain his silence. We both knew of his interest in poetry and his deep curiosity about topics connected to his Mexican heritage. It was difficult, at times, to reconcile his decision to remain quiet in school with his clear engagement in writing outside of the classroom. His involvement in learning and writing rarely seemed connected to school learning (Schultz, 2003).

Engagement and Disengagement

Until Luis spoke at the conclusion of this conversation, I failed to see the power that resided in his choice to remain silent. I saw his initial silence as an indication of reluctance to participate in the discussion, rather than a sign of his reflective thinking about the topic and a possible hint of his decision to time his response to have a deeper impact on the conversation. Later, I understood that Luis was simultaneously disengaged and engaged in the class discussions. He was acting aloof, holding himself apart from the conversation, yet at the same time attentive and thinking about his classmates' comments and how he might respond to them. There are several possible explanations for his silence. At that time, neither his teacher nor I asked him to elaborate because our attention was elsewhere. Although I did not initially decide to study silence in this classroom, as I looked closely at the classroom dynamics, its importance became clear. Thus, it was only after reflecting on this scene from a distance that the power of his silence was clear to me as a researcher.

Luis's silence can be understood as a form of reflection and a desire to choose his words carefully. Alternatively, we can interpret his choice to speak infrequently as connected to his position as a Mexican American student in a school where there was ongoing tension between and among groups of Latino and African American students. Or it might be recognized as a rejection of the traditional curriculum in his school that left little room for the study of Mexican Americans. Luis may have simply been uninterested in the conversation until this moment. Finally, his response can be understood as a self-protective refusal to engage in the complicated racial and cultural dynamics of the classroom, rather than a refusal to participate in its academic activities (Schultz, 2008). There is not a simple or even a single explanation. The effect of his decision, however, was to draw his classmates' attention to his comment, which allowed him to use silence as power.

I can offer several possible interpretations for Luis's silence that draw on daily field notes and interviews and take into account my sociocultural understandings of the local context and this moment in time. The critical point is that, whatever its intention, Luis's silence ended up being profoundly effective, creating the background against which his peers listened intently to his statement. By choosing to speak when he did, he seized control of the conversational floor at a critical moment. His contribution to that particular class was significant and more important than many days of inconsequential contributions. At the moment he made his argument out loud, the conversation became consequential for Luis. Arguments are most often won through the force of words, rather than through the power of silence. But in this instance, Luis's silence was a crucial element in the power of his argument and the course of the discussion.

Luis was born into a Mexican gang. His father, brothers, and extended family members all belonged to the same gang. In an interview, he explained that he wrote to stay alive. In his poetry, he wrote about the deep conflicts and emotions he experienced growing up and this writing helped him to express himself and keep a perspective on his life. Although he carried a few poems in his three-ring binder, he rarely showed these poems to his teachers or classmates. His stance toward school was to do the minimal amount of work needed to graduate (Schultz, 2003). He seemed to separate his work in school from the writing and talk that mattered most to him. Yet, on occasion, Luis would become intensely engaged in classroom discussions, dropping his typical stance of aloofness. In those instances, like the one described above, his classmates often paid close attention to his well-articulated position. For Luis, silence was punctuated by rare moments of speech rather than the reverse.

Luis was not asked by his teacher to explain his silence. She assumed that he was reluctant to participate in school. Until he spoke up at the conclusion of this conversation, the power that resided in his choice to remain silent was not apparent. Rather than simply framing his participation as disengagement or resistance, I suggest that he, like all students, was often both disengaged *and* engaged in discussions. A common assumption held by educators is that a student's persistent silence indicates his disengagement. Luis paid attention to the conversation and consciously chose when and how to vocally participate in the group discussion. While disengaged from the group discussion, he remained engaged in thought about the topic. At times, his statements were carefully timed and positioned to draw attention to themselves through the power of words and silence. Acting with agency, Luis chose when not to speak and when to speak by carefully paying attention to timing, registering disdain for certain topics and conversations. He strategically chose when to vocally participate in the classroom activities. Rather than claiming that Luis was silenced by his teachers, peers, or the institutional structures of his school or that he enacted a resistant stance, I suggest that his silence and his subsequent talk transformed the classroom conversation.

Attending only to talk masks the ways that silence can act as a sign of power that is integral to discourse. As Foucault (1977) explains:

> Silence itself . . . is less the absolute limit of discourse, the other side from which it is separated by a strict boundary, than an element that functions alongside the things said, with them and in relation to them within over-all strategies. . . . There is not one but many silences, and they are an integral part of the strategies that underlie and permeate discourses. (p. 27)

Foucault suggests that silences surround, undergird, and permeate speech. Rather than serving as a boundary for spoken words, silence is woven into speech and its meaning is indeterminate. Instead of focusing on either silence or talk, Foucault and others (e.g., Cage, 1961; Li, 2004; Sontag, 1969) urge us to see silence and talk as continuous. As the example of Luis illustrates, both silence and talk allow people to establish who they are in relation to others. Luis's participation can be characterized by his strategic use of silence, which lent power to his few words.

Political Resistance

Foley (1996) offers alternative explanations of the connections between silence and power. In his writing about Mesquaki students in predominantly White high schools, Foley challenges conventional anthropological and sociolinguistic explanations of the school failure of American Indians, which he claims ignore the phenomena of resistance and racism. Through his research, he found that White teachers perceived the "silent" stance of the Native students as indicative of their lack of motivation, and responded with low expectations that further exacerbated the negative interactions and silence. The less the teachers expected, the more the students seemed to withdraw. Younger students in this community were active and noisy. But by sixth grade, they began to pull back in school. The longer they stayed in school, Foley discovered, the more silent they became. In his conversations with the students, they explained their silence as a response to new and unfamiliar situations that were especially prevalent in their high school, which was located outside of the reservation. They worried about being laughed at if they did not have the correct answer. Their silence also reflected their anger, indifference, and boredom. Through extensive interviews, Foley concluded that the Mesquaki's silence had its roots in racial and political resistance in schools that were dominated and controlled by White administrators, teachers, and students.

The Mesquaki's decision to enact a silent stance was a self-assured political statement; in effect, it embodied power, while also disempowering them. But it is also critical to note that individual students made individual decisions. Foley found that some of the students were shy, others rebellious. Both responses to school looked the same: The students enacted silence. For all of the students, however, the price of silence was high, as many subsequently withdrew to the point that they left school before graduation. Their political resistance ended up hurting their life chances; although powerful in the moment, their silence left them with fewer options. It is likely that their teachers did not have the tools or knowledge about silence to seek to understand their choices. Grouped together and cast as "silent Indians" or, even worse, as "lazy and without ambition," their political statements went unheard by the school. The lesson for the teachers and adults in the community is to begin with the assumption that the silence has a purpose and meaning. Chapter 5 provides tools for such an exploration. If the teachers or adults recognize political resistance, they can sometimes redirect it toward learning and critical analysis. The students' silence may have embodied a powerful statement, but that statement led to less rather than more education.

Rethinking Voicelessness

In contrast to a view of silence as used strategically and initiated by students, educational research and writing often connects silence to student voicelessness. American Indians, Asian Americans, working-class girls, and gay students are a few of the subgroups who are often said to be "voiceless" in American schools, a term I find problematic because it does not account for forms of participation beyond speaking aloud. A focus on White middle-class girls who stop talking in middle school led researchers in the 1990s to claim that girls should be given a voice and empowered to participate in classrooms (e.g., Rogers, 1993; Taylor, Gilligan, & Sullivan, 1995). At times, there are serious consequences attendant on the decision to remain silent. Relational psychologists such as Gilligan (1982; see also Brown & Gilligan, 1992) found that when adolescent girls are faced with situations in which they feel obliged to conform to group norms that differ from their own, they frequently disavow or disconnect from their own beliefs and knowledge. This kind of silence is potentially harmful and can lead to a withdrawal from school and school-related activities (Raider-Roth,

2005). On the other hand, for some working-class students, such disconnection may be necessary to achieve school success (Walkerdine, Lucey,
& Melody, 2001). It is critical to distinguish and learn to identify various
kinds of student silences—silences of withdrawal, silences that are imposed,
and silences that allow students to remain engaged.

While students are often portrayed as silenced or rendered voiceless by
their peers, their teachers, and the institution of schooling, silence is rarely
understood as a form of maintaining and enacting a powerful and agentive
stance reflective of cultural traditions or individual choice. Knowing when
and how to be silent in a particular classroom governed by a set of rules
that are generally implicit can be as important as knowing when and how
to talk. Understanding the power of talk and silence is critical for successful
participation in classrooms. People tend to act based on a deeply internal-
ized set of rules that guide talk and silence in every day interactions.

Philips (1972, 1983) reports that Warm Springs Indians developed a
sophisticated understanding of timing, status, and relationship before they
spoke in school. Many mainstream students know the set of rules that
undergird classroom interaction. It is only when these rules clash or differ
for students located outside of the mainstream that the silence becomes
noticeable. Rather than assuming that a teacher's role is to empower students to speak, it may be more useful to make the classroom rules for silence and talk more explicit. Enacting a silent stance may be powerful in
the moment for the student. It may also lead to unintended consequences.
This choice is important for students to understand as they decide when
and how to speak or remain silent.

A focus on silence as well as talk highlights how the act of choosing
silence enables some individuals to hold onto and transmit power. It also
emphasizes the ways that Western traditions rely on speech rather than
silence to signify presence. The term *strategic silence* (Goldberger, Tarule,
Clinchy, & Belenky, 1996) refers to instances when individuals deliberately
choose to be silent. For instance, Basso (1979) reports that the Western
Apache used silence to exclude White outsiders. Quakers choose to integrate silence into their daily practices, including their decision making, as
a means of action and political protest rather than passivity (Baumann,
1983). Women's refusal to participate in a male-dominated discourse, at
times, is a form of silence and power (Gal, 1991). Likewise, feminist teachers' uses of silence can be understood as "an active transformative practice" (Lewis, 1993, p. 3). Lewis describes women's double-edged discourse
of speaking and silence as integral to feminist practice, concluding, "Our
speech is measured in silence" (p. 134). Whether intended or not, holding onto silence before speaking often allows a person to be heard. In other
circumstances, as with the Mesquaki Indians (Foley, 1996), it can lead to

misunderstanding and miseducation. With broader conceptions of silence and tools for investigating its meanings, teachers are better equipped to respond to the power in some students' silence.

Responding to Silence as Power

An understanding of silence as power raises several questions for teachers, including:

- How can we understand the uses of silence and talk in the context of both individual choices and identity categories?
- When do we accept silence as a form of participation, and when do we push students to speak so that their voices are added to the classroom discussion?
- How does our attention (and lack of attention) to silence highlight and even mask the interactional and power dynamics of our classrooms?
- How can we use silence to prompt conversations about how and when students choose to participate through both talk and silence?

If, by coding participation as speech, his teacher graded Luis on class participation each day, Luis might have accumulated a string of failing grades. If she graded him on the overall value of his contributions to the education of the class during the semester, along with his interest and knowledge of the subject, he would have done well. Ultimately, Luis participated in the classroom through silence as well as talk. As all comedians know, well-timed comments have the power to turn heads and make an impact. In Luis's case, the timing of his statement garnered his peers' attention and lent power and force to his contribution. Educators need better ways to recognize certain types of silence as participation—moments when students are engaged but not speaking out loud and moments when a few well-chosen words have considerable impact. At the same time, educators should be wary of assuming participation. Silence might simply mean disengagement. Luis may have been distracted or "checked out" for weeks for personal reasons, rather than biding his time and waiting for a powerful moment to speak. In this case, talk, whether powerful or not, can signal reengagement and participation.

What would it mean for educators to conceptualize classroom discourse as containing both talk and silence? How would that notion change how we understand students like Luis as engaged or disengaged? Silence is no more or no less powerful than talk; rather, it depends on the circumstance. The analysis of silence as a signifier of power illuminates and deepens our understanding of classroom participation to include more than verbal responses. A teacher might extend his understanding of Luis's participation by counting Luis's silent engagement in the discussions, looking at his nonverbal contributions, including his writing and informal conversations, and giving weight to comments that deepen the discussion rather than simply counting any kind of talk as participation. Conceptualizing Luis's silence and talk as forms of participation allows us to reexamine our assessment of students' roles and contributions to classroom discourse and learning.

Silence can signal a response to or an assertion of power. When a person responds to a question or statement with silence, that silence might be ignored or, conversely, it might attain significance. In the IRE sequence, a standard model of teacher-student question and response, teachers evaluate a student's response through talk (with a response such as "right") or through silence (and no response at all). A teacher's silence after a student's answer is its own evaluation and contains meaning (Jeff Shultz, personal communication, June 2007). The message may be contained in the physical positioning or facial expression of the teacher. Or it may be embedded in the silence itself and what the silence signifies in the classroom space.

When a teacher calls on a student who responds with silence, the student can be said to hold power. As a consequence of this interaction, the teacher may become frustrated at her inability to engender a response from the student. Most teachers believe they have few ways to convince a student to speak except through grades, negative evaluations, and threats. And those techniques only work for some students. I suggest that rather than threats or pleas, a teacher can seek to understand a student's silence in order to craft a response. Convincing a student to speak is not the only tactic available to teachers; understanding what the silence may signify is a useful starting point for a conversation or co-investigation. Conceptualizing silence as a part of a system that includes circulating models of how to be a student allows a teacher to understand how a student fits into the categories or models of identity available in the classroom and shaped by peers and teachers (Wortham, 2006).

SILENCE AS PROTECTION

Like many of her African American peers who lived in the city, Zakiya took on sometimes demanding responsibilities once she returned home from school. In addition to her mother, who she claimed was more of a peer, there were friends and neighbors, children and older people alike, who depended on her care. Yet these roles and responsibilities were not well understood by many of her teachers. One day a teacher demanded to know why she was in class without a pencil and notebook. Zakiya replied that she did not have money that week for a pencil. Her teacher replied, "Well go and babysit then to earn enough money to buy one." Zakiya had responsibility for childcare nearly every afternoon; like many of her low-income peers, she was not paid for this work. She answered the teacher with silence and a scowl. Zakiya was failing her eighth grade year and dropped out of school not long afterwards. (Schultz, 2003)

Drawn from a longitudinal study of middle school students just after desegregation mandates were lifted from a suburban district, this brief vignette illustrates one of many ways students might choose silence as a form of protection. Zakiya's mostly White and middle class teachers and peers knew little about her life at home, her goals, or her aspirations, which she hid behind her silence. Zakiya seemed to enact a stance of silence to protect her family and community life, which was not well understood by others in the school community. It may have been necessary for her to keep parts of her life hidden and outside of their gaze. From classroom observations and interviews with the teachers conducted over 2 years, we concluded that the teacher interpreted Zakiya's response as another example of her stubbornness and resistance. But in fact, at this point in the year, Zakiya informed us that she was working hard to re-engage in school. Circumstances and assumptions seemed to work against her. It may have been necessary for the teachers to respect Zakiya's need to remain silent about aspects of her home life, especially in the public spaces of her classroom.

A common response to student silence is to urge teachers to "give voice to students," insisting that they speak in public and contribute their ideas to the public discourse. This can be important in creating classrooms as democratic spaces. Educational scholars highlight the importance of student voice in reconceptualizing teaching, learning, and schooling (cf., Cook-Sather, 2002, 2006). I suggest that silence can be understood as a form of student voice and urge teachers to understand the broader context of how and why a student might choose to enact silence and, when appropriate, to build trusting relationships with students that lead to more opportunities for learning in school. Voice has several meanings. It can mean the vocalization of ideas out loud and it can refer to the incorporation of student ideas and perspectives in teaching and learning. Here, I refer to the latter understanding and suggest that silence is a critical aspect of student voice and participation, which may be vocal and may be silent.

Silence is not an individual attribute. Zakiya was not a shy person; in the lunchroom and among her friends, she was loud and boisterous. Her family, community, school, and classroom contexts, along with her interactions with teachers and classmates and the available practices and identities she had to choose from, led to her decisions to take on the mantle of silence in this particular moment. As she explained in a later interview, her silence was a form of protection.

While most scholarly research focuses on the hazards of silence for student success (e.g., Carter, 2001; Raider-Roth, 2005; Taylor, Gilligan, & Sullivan, 1995), the instrumental purposes for silence are rarely acknowledged. For instance, students are sometimes silent to protect their intelligence; they may choose to be silent (or, more accurately, quiet) as a form of camouflage. In some contexts, a student may choose silence or compromise over an overt display of intelligence in order to hold onto her popular status (Schultz, 2003). This inevitably leads to negative consequences.

In contrast to how silence sometimes impedes the academic progress of students—especially White middle-class girls—in her study of successful girls at an urban high school that was majority African American, Fordham (1993) describes how high-achieving African American girls became successful by adopting a silent stance. She explains:

> The most salient characteristic of the academically successful females at Capital High is a deliberate silence, a controlled response to their evolving, ambiguous status as academically successful students. Consequently, silence as a strategy for academic success at Capital is largely unconscious. Developing and using this strategy at the high school level enables high-achieving African-American females to deflect the latent and not too latent hostility and anger that might be directed at them were they to be both highly visible and academically successful. (p. 17)

Zakiya used silence primarily as protection against the institutional practices of her school. In contrast, the young women in Fordham's study used silence to become students who were perceived by the institution as successful. Fordham explains that the high-achieving girls appeared afraid to speak because their speech would draw attention to themselves. They learned that they could change others' perceptions through silence. As a result, they learned to act "as if absent rather than present" in class (p. 21). These unconscious actions allowed them to successfully navigate the institution of school.

In contrast to Zakiya's experience, Fordham concludes that in this high school, girls were prepared through silence for the difficulties they would encounter in their future lives negotiating family, conflicts, and academic success:

Regrettably, the high-achieving females at Capital High do not discern that their mothers and their seemingly unsupportive teachers are often unconsciously preparing them for a life away from the black community, a life in which they are the "doubly-refracted 'other.'" As the "doubly-refracted 'other'" the African-American female's survival "out there" is largely dependent upon her ability to live a life saturated with conflict, confusion, estrangement, isolations, and a plethora of unmarked beginnings and endings, jump starts, and failures. It is also likely to be a life in which a family of procreation and connections takes a back seat to "makin' it." (p. 24)

The African American girls were prepared by the adults in their lives and their predominantly Black school to learn silence in order to succeed academically and move away from their community for their education. At the same time, it was a perilous choice. Silence has different meanings in different local contexts and at different time periods. Fordham explains further that silence enacted by the high-achieving African American females is a deliberate act of defiance and a rejection of the low expectations of school officials. She likens learning silence to gender passing. Choosing to remain silent allowed the girls to remain invisible and thus "pass" relatively unharmed in their schools while learning to navigate future institutions. This interpretation of silence runs contrary to the assumptions made by most teachers and researchers that silence is simply stubborn resistance disconnected from a social analysis and adds to the portrait of Denise's resistance described above.

It may be the use of silence as survival that bell hooks (1989) writes about when she describes how she was taught silence as a child. She declares that she "was taught that it was important to speak but to talk a talk that was in itself a silence." As a child, she was punished for speaking:

There was no "calling" for talking girls, no legitimized rewarded speech. The punishments I received for "talking back" were intended to suppress all possibility that I would create my own speech. That speech was to be suppressed so that the "right speech of womanhood" would emerge. (pp. 5–6)

Learning silence as a child was meant to ensure her ability to survive as a Black female in and out of school. Through practice, she developed a silent voice that allowed her to communicate.

Hong Kingston (1989) writes about a similar experience from the perspective of a recent Asian American immigrant:

Normal Chinese women's voices are strong and bossy. We American-Chinese girls had to whisper to make ourselves American-feminine. . . . Some of us gave up, shook our heads, and said nothing, not one word. Some of us could not even shake our heads. . . . We invented an American-feminine speaking personality, except for that one girl who could not even speak up in Chinese school. (p. 172)

To succeed in school, rather than imitating boys, Hong Kingston and her peers copied the "American" (White) girls by adopting a stance of silence. Ironically, this stance of silence became attached as an identity only for the Asian American girls, separating them further from their White peers. Understanding silence as a property of Asian Americans, Whites, or Blacks fails to take into account the historical and sociopolitical moment. In Wortham's (2006) terms, among the available publicly circulating models of being a student for the new Chinese immigrants were models of silent students. Their teachers and peers participated in this process of constructing them as silent. This interpretation developed over time and became a stereotyped Asian American way of doing school. Duncan (2004) explains that in Hong Kingston's memoir, *Woman Warrior*, "speech and silence are conceptualized as gendered means of communication, shaped by subject position, immigration status, and sanity" (p. 25). I would add that speech and silence are also shaped by classroom contexts and larger sociocultural patterns.

Writing of the need to transform silence into action, Lorde (1984) explains, "My silences have not protected me. Your silence will not protect you" (p. 41). Lorde (1997) believed that silence masked fear and, further, that it was essential to confront this fear, an idea she elaborates in her poem "Litany for Survival":

> and when we speak we are afraid
> our words will not be heard
> nor welcomed
> but when we are silent
> we are still afraid.
>
> (p. 256)

It is critical to imagine conditions under which youth would choose to speak rather than remain fearful and silent and, conversely, conditions under which youth do not, and perhaps should not, speak. In the short time that we are in this world, Lorde suggests, we need to choose how we use our voice in order to survive or fully live.

Understanding the decision to invoke silence can open up possibilities for rethinking student participation. Schools and classrooms are often filled with ridicule and rejection. Youth, especially adolescents, often choose to be silent or withdraw from a situation to protect themselves from these behaviors (Bosacki, 2005; Finders, 1996). Their silence is not simply an individual choice but one constructed in relation to their teachers, peers, and the interactional contexts of their classrooms, schools, and wider society. Zakiya's silence and the silence of the girls in Fordham's study essentially allowed them to remain invisible. How might that same silence be reconfigured as a presence that comes with protection? Teachers can begin by establishing classrooms that emphasize relationship and trust (Raider-Roth, 2005). Further, they can provide ways for students to speak through silence and to be heard in ways that appear safer to them (if not completely safe.) Understanding the dangers of speaking—and of remaining silent—is integral to teaching *all* students. Reading silence as the need for protection, respecting the need—at times—to refrain from speech, is equally difficult and important.

SILENCE AS A RESPONSE TO TRAUMA

Many youth, especially those in urban and rural settings, have experienced some kind of trauma, including abuse, experiences related to immigration, and conditions associated with abject poverty, among other causes. As a result of trauma, youth often find themselves without words to describe their circumstances, frequently falling into silence. Rogers (2006) opens her book about psychotherapy with children who have experienced serious trauma with the following description of her own response to trauma during adolescence:

> I stood on the porch. Dark mesh screens rose fifteen feet high, divided by thin black iron poles that parceled the sky into parallelograms. Above me a ledge stuck out its tongue, dark and square, and made a long shadow all along one side of the porch. I had not spoken for over a month. I stood on the porch and saw everything in sharp relief. The silence pressed in on me and opened up with sound: keys in a remote hallway, feet shuffling on linoleum, a squirrel's scuffle across the bare ground into leaves three stories below. Nothing was expected of me. I lay down on a battered couch and studied the sky. (p. 3)

Rogers (2006) explains that she stopped speaking for 5 months when she was 16 as a result of traumatic events in her family that led her to worry that what she might say would be misconstrued. For her, silence was both protest and protection. Through her silence, she protested engagement with others. Rogers's silence protected her from the world that threatened to be unkind and misunderstand her, providing her with a place to retreat. In addition to protection, her silence came from an inability to find words that were adequate to convey the events that had transpired in her life.

This experience of being without adequate words occurs on a different scale in classrooms as well. At times, it coincides with a need for protection, a concept explored above, and at other times, it arises from a sense that words cannot adequately capture and convey an emotion, idea, or experience connected to trauma, the focus of this section. Sometimes the two are tightly intertwined. People find themselves without words in response to trauma or difficult situations they may not be able to convey with words alone. Silence is often connected to painful memories and, at times, holds a place for them.

Rogers (2006) writes about the location of silence in her work with adolescents who struggle with trauma related to abuse. She explains, "For me each and every word holds the unsayable—and all language requires translation" (p. 294). Put differently, all words also contain silences. Through translation, some language might be transposed into nonverbal signals—facial expressions, shrugs, shifts in position, or silence—while other aspects of language may more easily be translated into verbal and recognizable signs. Rather than insisting that all language be translated into verbal contributions to public discourse, I urge teachers to learn to read students' silences, recognizing that ideas, feelings, and contributions may be hidden within them.

Silence can be a container for thoughts, memories, and events that are difficult to put into words. Conditions may change, allowing people to speak, although a teacher's goal is not simply to bring a student into speech. There are countless instances related to the lives of children when traumatic events have occurred—and continue to occur—to individuals and groups of people. Often, these events are left out of history, representing a particular kind of silence and a form of silencing. For participants of the events, they are often too traumatic to put into words; they are unspeakable.

Writing about the internment of American citizens of Japanese descent in the United States during World War II, for instance, Yamamoto (1994, in Duncan, 2004) describes a strategy used by Japanese American women who wore "masks" of silence. She explains, "Inaugurated by the trauma of the racially marked, gendered, and sexualized body's positioning in the social economy of the United States, masking is a resistant strategy by which the body and, through the body, subjectivity may be claimed" (pp. 100–101). The women used silence to resist and hide as a way to claim their selfhood.

Silence is connected to memory, including historical memories. Maclear (1994) explicates a film and oral history made by an Asian Canadian about the experiences of the Japanese Canadians in the internment camps during World War II. She writes that the pauses and unedited silences in the film represent "the lapses and disjunctures attendant in processes of remembering" (p. 9). While others found these gaps disconcerting, Maclear found them revealing, explaining, "They guided me to what he was not telling and reminded me that some things will always remain unspoken— and unknowable" (p. 9). Although students may not be able to put their memories into words, it is likely that memories have a presence in their lives and in the classroom.

Stein (2004) posits that memories are sometimes stored in the body: "Bodies hold history, memory, thought, feeling, and desires. Bodies hold language and silence. Our bodies are repositories of knowledge, but these knowledges are not always knowable in and through language—they can be felt, imagined, imaged or dreamed" (p. 99). We store ideas that are impossible to put into words in our bodies; they are encased in silence that is rarely translated into words spoken aloud. The teacher's task is not to coerce the student to reveal these memories but to notice their presence and provide conditions that support learning and growth. Many educators may not be as easily guided to the gaps as Maclear or as attuned as Stein to noticing the physical presence of silence. The recognition that silence or gaps in speech may contain important content that remains hidden, however, is a place to begin.

There are always unspeakable and unknowable aspects of students' lives connected to trauma and leading to silence. As MacKendrick (2001) explains:

> Many of us scoff at the ineffable, at the very possibility of ineffability and assume that whereof one cannot speak one is simply inadequately educated and articulate—or lying. . . . [However, these] matters are more complex: . . . within even the most articulate speaking there murmurs the loss of meaning, the coming of absence which is silence. (p. 4)

As MacKendrick describes, at times silence signifies the ineffable. Some memories, feelings, and ideas exist beyond a person's ability or desire to translate them into spoken words.

In a discussion about their efforts to respond to apartheid and racial discrimination in their country through multimodalities, a group of South African girls explained, "Sometimes we run out of words, but not out of body language" (Stein & Newfield, 2002). For some people and in certain instances, words do not contain the meanings and feelings they seek to communicate. In addition, the process of putting ideas and events into spoken or written words may be too painful. Alternative forms of expression, including new modalities, as I describe in Chapter 4, can provide people with opportunities to convey feelings, knowledge, and ideas. Understanding the limits of spoken and written texts—especially when students have experienced trauma—as well as the constraints of the classroom context,

allows teachers and researchers to reframe silence as an active and strategic choice rather than as a passive response.

In Cha's *Dictee* (1995), silence is a way of telling a different story.
Cha juxtaposes textual silences with more public forms of silencing, illustrating how the limitations of the language available to us render some
ideas "unspeakable" or incomprehensible. As Duncan (2004) explains,
"To unsay, for Cha, involves a careful acknowledgement of that fact that
she writes—and lives—under constant threat of erasure" (p. 219). Many
youth live under the threat of becoming invisible in classrooms and
schools. Fighting to become visible—or, conversely, to remain invisible—
they make daily choices about when to speak and when to remain silent
(Brayboy, 2004). As Campano (2007) explains, silence is a presence that
shifts according to context and time.

There are various responses for teachers and students when presented
with this challenge of representing or conveying the unspeakable. In schools,
as described in Chapter 4, a teacher might attempt to provide space, various
modalities, and materials to represent the unsayable, allowing students to
communicate through other modalities while also giving them the opportunity to protect themselves and their stories through silence (Schultz, Buck,
& Niesz, 2005; Schultz & Coleman, 2009). As another example, in the school
referred to earlier, where the desegregation order had been recently re-
scinded (e.g., Schultz, Buck, & Niesz, 2000), a multiracial group of students
wrote a play about their experiences with race and racism in their middle
school. After reading it aloud, they erased some of their stories, softening
the language and adding silence. They realized that the audience for the
play would include their peers, which made some of the lines in the play,
in their words, "unsayable" (Schultz, Buck, & Niesz, 2005). They chose to
represent some of their experiences and emotions through silence rather
than words, using the words in the text to hold only pieces of their reality.

As part of this same research project, we held conversations about race
and racism in the school with separate groups of White and Black students
(the two dominant racial groups in the school) before initiating what we
called "mixed-race" group discussions. Students informed us that there
were stories, feelings, and ideas that they could talk about in the single
race groups but not in the mixed-race setting. In the latter context, the
stories were expressed through silence (Schultz, Buck, & Niesz, 2000).

Writing about the evolution of the English language, Spender (1980)
explains the role of patriarchy in the limitations on women's speech. Rich
(1979) makes a similar point in her essay "Taking Women Seriously":

> Look at the many kinds of women's faces, postures, expressions. Listen to the
> women's voices. Listen to the silences, the unasked questions, the blanks. Listen

to the small, soft voices, often courageously trying to speak up, voices of women taught early that tones of confidence, challenge, anger, or assertiveness, are strident and unfeminine. Listen to the voices of the women and the voices of the men: observe the space men allow themselves, physically and verbally, the male assumption that people will listen, even when the majority of the group is female. Look at the faces of the silent, and of those who speak. Listen to a woman groping for language in which to express what is on her mind, sensing that the terms of academic discourse are not her language, trying to cut down her thought to the dimensions of a discourse not intended for her. (pp. 243–244)

First-generation women university students, Rich asserts, are forced to speak in a language that is foreign to them and does not easily accommodate their ideas and experiences. Further, they are placed in classrooms that are hostile to their attempts at these formulations. In the decades following the statements made by Spender and Rich, feminist studies focused on girls and women who were thought to lack a voice (Walkerdine, 1990). Explaining that both silence and talk are regulated, Walkerdine asserts that women's silence represents "psychic repression, suppression of the articulation of forbidden discourse" and political resistance (p. 30). There are some ideas that are ineffable, not easily expressed through words either because of the nature of the idea or the limitation of language (Van Manen, 1990). Silence occurs when people lack the words to speak because of the circumstances of their lives, including when they have experienced difficult or traumatic events in their lives and language is not adequate. Responding to students who lack words, teachers can shift their pedagogy and curriculum. It may not be necessary, appropriate, or safe for students to tell their traumatic stories, rather teachers can give them time and space to express themselves through silence and other modalities.

In Chapter 4, I describe curricular methods that enable students to express themselves in modalities other than text, allowing them to move beyond words to tell stories. If the students in the desegregated school I studied had been given alternatives to written text, they might have found modalities—pictures or music, for instance, in addition to text—to express their ideas, instead of erasing the words. In addition, rather than assuming that all students will talk in equal amounts, classrooms can be organized to hold spaces for silence, recognizing and valuing ideas expressed in silence as well as those expressed in words said aloud. In order to participate through silence, a student has the responsibility of communicating ideas even without vocalization. At the same time, the teacher and classmates have the responsibility to create conditions for engaged participation through silence. Chapter 5 provides examples of tools for classroom teachers to recognize these kinds of silences (see also Raider-Roth, 2005).

SILENCE AS A TIME AND SPACE FOR
CREATIVITY AND LEARNING

> The stupendous reality is that language cannot be understood unless
> we begin by observing that speech consists, above all, in silences.
> (Ortega y Gassett, 1957)

Gallas (1998) describes a 6-year-old student, Rachel, from her own first-grade classroom, who was completely silent for months and would not participate in any public conversations in the classroom. Rachel simply refused to respond to teacher or student questions about any topic. Nothing seemed to engage her verbally in classroom activities. She was only willing to work with one classmate who was learning English and also relatively silent. They exchanged only a few words when they worked or played together. Because of her own history, Gallas understood that girls who take a silent stance are often considered "good" and overlooked. Rachel's silence allowed her to control the relationships and discourse around her, giving her power. Her silence was a discursive strategy. She used this strategy successfully to shape her interactions with her peers, as well as her interactions with her teacher. Gallas believed that Rachel's silence enabled her to exercise as much power as the noisy "bad" boys in the class. When the boys were disruptive, Gallas could ask them to leave the classroom. In contrast, Gallas was unable (or unwilling) to punish Rachel for her silence.

Gallas began to learn to read Rachel's shrugs and gestures as forms of communication akin to talk. Even so, she kept gently pressuring Rachel to speak and contribute to the public discourse of the classroom. Eventually, through studying Rachel's silence, Gallas came to understand that it functioned not just as a strategy for exercising power, but as a container for her vivid imagination. She saw that Rachel was guarding her private world with silence. One day during recess, after a heroic effort to save her friend from sinking into mud on the playground, Rachel broke her classroom silence to breathlessly tell the story to the assembled class. After that incident, she spoke in school, shifting the relationship between her silence and her imaginative worlds and renegotiating her decision to remain silent. Whereas inhabiting her imaginary worlds once had been contingent on Rachel's silence, she was able to hold onto these worlds as she began to talk in school. It may have been that she needed to trust her classmates and her teachers before she was willing and able to leave the protected space of her imagination.

Gallas decided that Rachel had taken a silent stance in the classroom in order to create a space for her imagination and nurture her creativity.

Few teachers would have responded to Rachel with Gallas's patience. It often seems too difficult to teach a student who surrounds herself in complete silence and does not outwardly respond to the teacher. But rather than refusing to allow the young girl's silence or assuming it had negative connotations, Gallas studied it, discerning its meaning and waiting for Rachel to choose to shift her mode of participation in the public arena. She understood her silence as participation—although she did not frame it as such—and Rachel was included as an active member of the classroom community. As a consequence, Rachel was granted time and space to enter the classroom on her own terms. She was able to become a recognized and verbal participant of the classroom community while still retaining her imaginative life.

In contrast to Rachel, who took an extreme stance toward silence, most students engage in silence in a more moderate fashion. Students may participate in silence because they retreat to their imaginations. Alternatively, they may enact a silent stance because they want or need more time to think through ideas. Rapid-paced classrooms privilege students who can respond quickly and accurately (preferably with the teacher's answer); other participants may need time to reflect and the opportunity to try out ideas in small groups or through writing. It may be necessary for teachers to learn to read students' nods and facial expressions to understand silence as a form of participation, and to understand that students who are silent may be as engaged in learning as the student who speaks frequently, dominating the floor. As teachers, we can ask ourselves how and whether we accommodate students who take more time to respond and formulate thoughts by considering the following questions among others:

- What roles do we—and their classmates—assign these students as members of the classroom community?
- Given the press of tests and covering material, what are the values we exhibit in classrooms in terms of speed and deliberation?
- How do we make room for silence and thoughtfulness, and when are these opportunities foreclosed?
- Do we encourage students to guess at answers, offering incorrect and incomplete thoughts in order to gain the teacher's recognition, rather than supporting careful (and sometimes slower and more deliberate) thinking?

In addition to fostering creativity, silence is often critical for language learning and reflection. When students learn a new language, there is often a period of silence. A person may not speak or produce the new language at first because he is still listening and absorbing it. Not everyone goes through this silent period, and it lasts for varied amounts of time. Whether or not someone goes through a period of not speaking when learning a new language does not seem connected to later proficiency in the language. Silence seems necessary for some but not all language learners (Granger, 2004). The space created by the silence provides language learners with time to develop skills and to draw on creative resources. How do educators give monolingual or second-language learners this time and space? What does it look like in classrooms to provide additional time for students?

Granger (2004) tells the story of a 5-year-old boy who arrived in Toronto with little knowledge of English. He was placed in an all-English-speaking kindergarten. Without success, his teacher tried to encourage him to speak, offering him a variety of materials and activities. He remained completely silent. One day, the class went on a fieldtrip to the zoo. When the boy saw a reticulated python wrapped several times around a branch inside a glass display case, he dragged his teacher over to the case, speaking his first words aloud in English, "Me know this! Me know this! This my home, teacher, this my home!" (p. x)

In this striking example, a child waited until he was ready to speak and had something to say before uttering his first words to his teacher. He had great motivation to speak in this particular moment, and as a result, he spoke several sentences. We expect silence when a person (whether child or adult) is learning a new language. This same silence is useful for learning new concepts or processing new ideas in classrooms. Silence can give students control over their learning and time to learn new material at their own pace. The amount of time that a student needs might be highly individual, suggesting that enforced silence when students are working on a project may be useful to some but not all students. It is telling that both Gallas's student and this 5-year-old spoke their first words when they had something urgent to communicate to others and a message that was highly personal. There was authenticity in their need to communicate. Through telling their stories, they may have become more engaged in classroom learning. How often do students feel a sense of urgency in U.S. classrooms and classrooms around the world? How much time is spent practicing for tests, learning skills that have little relevance and urgency to the rest of their lives?

For English Language Learners, trauma can play a compounding role in the silent space required for students to learn and use a new language. Campano (2007) describes this phenomenon as "necessary silences." Student silences may keep a teacher from knowing her students. On the other hand, the silences may be necessary for the student to move forward. Campano introduces a student in his classroom, Ma-Lee, a recent Hmong immigrant who initially struggled to succeed in school in traditional ways.

In addition to learning the cultural practices and norms of her new school, she struggled to express her ideas in a second language. During the first month of school, Campano writes, her silence was a "felt presence" (p. 65). Her only words were those spoken softly to a peer who was also Hmong. By giving her time to find words, Campano respected her decision to remain silent.

Early in the year, Campano created a space he called a "second classroom" where, before and after school and during lunch, students joined him in informal conversations about issues important to their lives. In this space, which had different norms for participation, Ma-Lee began to speak openly about her painful experiences, which she ultimately wrote about in her "Autobiography of a Hmong Girl" (Campano, 2007). She may have needed more time and a different kind of space to develop the academic literacies to participate in the classroom discourse and complete standard assignments. The time, the different participation structures of this space, and its intimacy allowed her to develop language to communicate her experiences and thoughts. Her silence was not a permanent condition or even an individual characteristic. Instead, it was a temporary stance until, as a new English Language Learner, she found the words to express her experiences and felt safe enough to participate in the classroom through writing.

People can be silent when they are literally caught between two languages as Hymes (1967, in McDermott, 1988) explains through the story of a Menomeni Indian, White-Thunder. Without access to the words he needed, White-Thunder chose silence. White-Thunder was only described as inarticulate in relation to others who spoke more fluently, in relation to particular languages and rules that governed them. These same situations exist in schools; students' inarticulateness is often masked by or read as silence. McDermott (1988) describes how classrooms are organized around "inarticulateness." As long as we insist that some people, like White-Thunder, are inarticulate while others are deemed articulate, classrooms sort students into those categories, among others. McDermott concludes, "In working for conditions that organize our own articulateness, we cannot afford to make others systematically inarticulate" (p. 47).

People are often silent when they are learning a new way of acting or norms for behavior. Even members of the "mainstream" have this experience. In the 1990s, Rogers and her colleagues (e.g., 1993) found that in middle school many of the White middle-class girls she observed and spoke with decided to become silent and stop articulating their feelings in order to learn what is acceptable among their peers. Researchers found that during adolescence White middle-class girls explore the relationship between public silence and their inner voices, developing what Rogers calls "psychological resistance—the disconnection of one's own experiences from consciousness" (p. 289). A purely psychological exploration of this phenomenon focuses on the girls' internal decisions to remain silent. An alternative and sociocultural explanation also focuses attention on the social context, which may feel unsafe for experimentation, as well as the peer group and the available models for acting like a White, middle-class girl. These decisions—to remain silent or to speak—are contingent and individual, but always guided by group and societal norms. At times, students need space and time for reflection and learning. Rather than "giving students voice," teachers can create structures that give students the latitude they need to learn and create. As I describe in Chapter 3, teachers can weave time for silent reflection into busy, regulated schooldays as well as into individual interactions with their students. In addition, teachers can shift their expectations of participation and change their classroom structures, roles, and formats to open up their understandings of the contributions students make through silence.

CONCLUSION: EXPANDING OUR FRAMEWORKS

This chapter offers new frameworks to extend understandings of how students enact silence in the classroom. Yet the analysis it proffers leaves educators with the dilemma of when to accept silence as participation, providing space for it in classrooms, and, alternatively, when to create conditions to promote speech so that students are a part of the public discourse. The definition of classroom participation proposed in Chapter 1— contributions to a group activity that create and extend the spaces for understanding—provides educators with a rubric for distinguishing between engaged participation and disengagement, and suggests the following questions about the role of silence and participation:

- How much responsibility to the group does an individual have to speak and contribute to the conversation?
- How much responsibility to the individual does the group have to protect her right to hold onto silence?
- When are silences acceptable, even necessary, and when do they foreclose learning for either the individual or the group?
- When does an individual's silence help him learn despite other obstacles, such as a peer group that does not support or understand an academic focus?
- When does silence provide a space for a student to learn to adapt and adopt group norms or language and when does it signal a retreat and a refusal of engaged participation?

- When is a student's silence a powerful contribution and when does that powerful statement come too late or in a form that a teacher or group is unable to hear or understand, disconnecting the student from the classroom activity?
- What tools are needed to read some silences as engaged participation that moves a discussion or activity forward and other silences as withdrawal or disengagement?

Writing about inarticulateness, McDermott (1988) explains: "The force of an utterance is rarely dependent simply on matters of form; it is not the utterance alone that makes a difference, as much as the conditions for its being delivered, heard, acted on, remembered, and quoted" (p. 41). Like talk, silence is best understood in its social context. Silence and inarticulateness are not always markers of powerlessness; they are socially, politically, historically, and culturally constructed in local contexts (Gal, 1991; McDermott, 1988). Silence can have a range of forms and functions in the classrooms. Students have a variety of reasons for enacting silence. They may take a silent stance because they do not feel as though they have anything important to say. Silence may be the most available model for acting in a classroom. It is often difficult to determine the exact meanings and functions of a student's silence (Lebra, 1987).

Silence is neither an individual trait nor a decision made by an individual alone. Some people are shy, but they tend to be shy in certain contexts, bold or talkative in others. Some people may choose to enact silence, but that silence is often simultaneously chosen for them. When our daughter was young, we used to say that she was quiet-loud: quiet at school, where she was reticent to contribute to classroom discussions; loud at home when she had to vie with her two siblings for space in the dinner table conversation. We were told that her quietness at school could become a liability for her in the future. With the advice of her teacher, we worked to offer her tools to participate more vocally in school. We enrolled her in an afterschool theater class to help her learn to speak more loudly and freely in public. Through that experience, she gained confidence to make more frequent verbal contributions to classroom conversations. In school, her voice became stronger, louder, and more self-assured. Later, she explained that she preferred to be judicious when she made contributions in class, waiting until she had something to say that was different or unique. She learned, however, that most of her teachers valued a raised hand and frequent verbal participation more than this judiciousness. As this example illustrates, my daughter learned when and how to speak up at school, and, as parents, we recognized the need to give her additional strategies. What would it have meant for her teachers to change their understandings of

what participation meant in their classrooms and to expand their understandings of "silent" students rather than expecting students to change?
What would it mean for all students to learn how to understand the value
and consequences of their decisions of when to remain silent and when
to talk?

To return to a prior example, Zakiya enacted a silent stance in her
classroom in response to a teacher's insistence that she buy a pencil. Over
time, this and many other seemingly nonacademic decisions may have had
serious consequences for her future in school. At the end of eighth grade,
she dropped out of school. Her reputation as a resistant and disengaged
student did not arise from a single incident, but rather from an accumula-
tion of moments when she refused to participate, withdrew from a class
activity or discussion, or simply remained silent when she was asked a
question. She did not consciously become a student who gradually withdrew from school, nor did her teachers consciously push her into that
position. In each moment, her response made sense. Likewise, her teacher's
reaction to Zakiya's defiant silence in the moment likely had its own logic
and fit into a set of expectations she had already formed of this student.
The problem does not lie in a single response to Zakiya; rather, it might
rest in teachers' lack of knowledge of and practice in how to understand
the possible meanings and functions of a student's silence. Had her teachers held a broader set of understandings of silence, they may have pos-
sessed more ways to engage Zakiya in school learning.

When there are silent students in classrooms, educators can ask
whether they are enacting group norms (e.g., a decision not to speak to
authorities out of deference or politeness or a decision not to offer obvi-
ous answers) or making individual decisions (e.g., to enact silence as a form
of resistance to school learning or to act out of boredom or anger) (Pollock, 2004). Whatever the initial explanation, it is critical to read or understand silence through a social and interactional lens and, through such
understandings, learn how and why a student might decide to enact a
particular form of silence at a particular time and place.

These understandings of how and why students might enact silence
open up more possibilities for understanding students' decisions in classrooms. A focus on silence and talk enables us to see and hear a student's
thinking and allows us to understand how a student is positioned to learn
in a classroom. Including silence as a form of participation allows us to
develop democratic practices that are more responsive to youth, providing greater opportunities for learning. In Chapter 3, I explore the ways
silence works at the classroom level with a focus on the uses of silence in
teaching.

Classroom Silences, Classroom Talk

The Room 110 Pledge
I am a beautiful child.
I come to school to learn.
I come to school to help myself.
I come to school to help my family.
I come to school to help my community.
I must respect myself.
I must respect my classmates.
I must respect my teachers.
I believe that I am a brilliant child.
I come from great people.
I come from great ancestors.
Imhotep, Nefertiti, Nat Turner, Frederick Douglass,
Harriet Tubman, Marcus Garvey,
Dr. King, Malcolm X, Fanny Lou Hamer, my parents.
I come from great people.

EACH MORNING during my fieldwork, the children in Mattie Davis's first-grade classroom recited these words affirming their pride in themselves and their race. After the chant, the students stood in silence for a few minutes. Their words rang true in this classroom, which was governed by rules and practices that reflected respect and admiration for each member of the classroom community. Located in a high-poverty neighborhood and a school that is "underperforming" according to the statewide tests and guidelines imposed by the No Child Left Behind Act, this classroom was generally noisy and filled with purposeful activity after the initial moment of silence following the pledge. Ms. Davis's voice could often be heard above the others, gently guiding children to their seats or the next activity. Her voice was simultaneously playful and affirming, firm and serious. The walls were covered with inspirational posters and student work; there were picture books crammed into shelves in a back corner designated for independent reading and class meetings, and several plants were located on a mobile cart along the edges of the room. Science experiments—seeds planted in Styrofoam cups—lined shelves next to the windows. The closets were filled with supplies carefully gathered over the years.

The students were generally seated in clusters of desks or rows that shifted according to the designated activity. When working on their individual workbooks or stories, they were usually quiet, leaving their seats or raising their voices primarily to ask questions. Ms. Davis organized her class so that while she worked with small groups, the rest of the children worked on their own. During these times, students often walked over to Ms. Davis with questions. She generally shooed them away, reminding them to ask their peers first for assistance. In general, there was a delicate balance between order and chaos, noise and silence. Children were engaged in their assigned work until they slipped into talk with their peers, and the teacher had to issue a reminder for silence and focus. Then the rhythm of focus and distraction, noise and relative quiet, resumed.

As Ms. Davis and her first graders recited the 110 pledge each morning, they were reminded of the rules for participation in the classroom. Contained in the pledge were implicit rules or norms of behavior. These rules guided classroom interaction, regulated talk and silence, and were integral to how teaching and learning occurred in this classroom.

Talk and silence are always present in relationship to each other in classrooms. We tend to focus on the talk—its presence or absence—rather than the silence. Shifting from a sole focus on talk to an examination of talk and silence together and investigating the relationship between the two modes of interaction allow a teacher to consciously structure classrooms that are more inclusive of all students. In this chapter, I analyze the use of structures that include silence and talk to build the case for counting silence as participation. Framing classroom interactions through silence and talk allows a teacher to see, hear, and understand students' learning in new ways.

Chapter 2 describes some of the ways that students enact silence in relationship to their larger lifeworlds, including classroom interactions. In this chapter, I focus on the rules for classroom participation and the ways various structures allow for and are shaped by different kinds and amounts of talk and silence. As in Chapter 1, I use the term *participation structure* to emphasize how classrooms are organized for teacher and student interaction (cf., Philips, 1972), which might include appropriating new roles, such as when a student takes on the teacher's role in a literacy activity called the Author's Chair. A focus on participation structures emphasizes that speaking—and refraining from speech—are actions that shape and are shaped by particular social relationships and contexts. I begin with a discussion of how silence can be integral to a teacher's pedagogical practices and student learning. I examine the rules for silence and talk in classrooms. Next, I explore the ways that teachers introduce silence or silent periods of time into their classrooms and, conversely, how teachers break silence through shifting the ways the classroom interactions are organized. Throughout this chapter, I use vignettes to represent patterns in Mattie Davis's classroom that illustrate the interrelationships among silence, talk, and classroom participation.

SILENCE AS INTEGRAL TO TEACHING AND LEARNING

Silence structures most interactions in classrooms, surrounding teachers' and students' questions and responses. Silence enables people to be heard in classrooms—such as a response to a question surrounded by silence— and defines participation in specific ways. Teachers often use variations on the IRE sequence to structure class participation in ways that meet their goals and respond to their students—for instance, changing who initiates the conversational turns in the classroom. The conversational sequences or structures that teachers use are characterized and shaped by different amounts of talk and silence and various rules for turn-taking. For instance, whole-group discussions generally depend on the silence of the group while an individual speaks. In most instances, the teacher controls the talk and silence, monitoring who has the opportunity to speak and who is expected to remain silent.

In a variation of this structure known as the Author's Chair, students are given the opportunity to initiate the conversational turns and read their own piece of writing. In this structure, the student author takes on a teacher's role and controls the talk and silence, calling on peers to offer their responses. When a student reads a story aloud to a group, our focus—as teachers and researchers—tends to be on the content of the story and the talk that surrounds it. The success or failure of the event—and the students—is often largely dependent on the talk that transpires. However, teaching and learning occur through both talk and silence. A focus on silence allows us to perceive new dimensions of instructional activity. Both silence and talk inform how students learn and how teachers teach. A close look at a single, representative activity illuminates how this happens.

Rules for Talk, Rules for Silence

It was April, near the end of the school year. The first graders had just finished their "facts" research papers on topics about which they had developed expertise. The research papers were written on plain white paper and stapled together into a book. After the group had gathered on the rug at the back of the room, Ms. Davis invited

a girl to read her story about her mother, ritually calling out her
signal for silence, "All eyes on me." The girl took the Author's
Chair and read her "facts" book with ease, while the class listened
in relative silence. After the girl concluded her story, Ms. Davis
asked the class to give her a "thumbs up"—their silent practice of
recognizing a peer. A few more students read their short books.

Terrell's hand shot up, and Ms. Davis called on him to be the
next reader. Terrell walked to the front of the room, sat on the
chair, opened his book, and read his title, "Being a Better Writer."
As he struggled with each word of the book, his classmates silently
came up to the chair and stood behind him. One by one, they each
helped him read the words on the page and then returned to their
seats. After she initially called on Terrell to read, Ms. Davis sat
quietly among the students, closely monitoring the scene without
saying a word.

Terrell began by looking at his teacher as he haltingly read each
word and sentence. When he came to a new word, he stopped,
waited for a classmate to mouth the word to him, and then cau-
tiously proceeded, taking the suggestions and support from his peers.
The scene the students created was like a silent dance: One by one,
students approached Terrell, stood alongside or behind him, and
offered their help, a new student silently slipping next to Terrell as
the previous one left. By the conclusion of the book, a small cluster
of students rose to surround Terrell in silence, offering support as he
read the final words.

Because Mattie Davis's classroom was usually loud and filled with
noisy activity, both the teacher's and the students' silences were notable
in this scene. Ms. Davis guided the students through silence. After initially
checking in with his teacher through a glance, Terrell accepted the help
of his peers, with silent assent. Without asking permission or verbally jock-
eying for space or the opportunity to help Terrell, his peers organized themselves to assist him, following an implicit set of classroom rules that guided
their respectful, gentle actions. The nonverbal orchestration of turns reflected the classroom norms of respect and the students' understanding of
the classroom routines. Verbal communication was kept to a minimum,
which allowed Terrell to maintain the floor as the author of his text.
Through the silence of the teacher and students, he was able to hold the
power and authority in this scene, despite his struggles as a reader and his
need for support. The classroom rules that undergirded this scene structured the students' interactions with one another and guided the teacher's
decisions as she sat on the sideline.

Much of the literature on silence in classrooms addresses teachers' acts of silencing students, analyzing the negative consequences of teacher-imposed student silence. In addition, teacher education textbooks and research suggest that teachers intentionally add silence to classrooms through what is commonly called "wait time" (Rowe, 1986), or an insistence on silence while one person is talking (usually the teacher) or while students are working on their own. This vignette suggests a different interpretation and use of silence in the classroom. Through silent participation in this classroom and a set of rules for behavior, the teacher and students collectively supported a struggling reader to become an author. Teachers use silence in classrooms in a wide variety of ways, sometimes intentionally and at other times seamlessly woven into daily activities. In this scene, Ms. Davis created conditions for student participation through rules that guided the use of silence and talk. In addition, her silence allowed students to participate in several different ways, including through silence. Ms. Davis's silence allowed Terrell to read his own story and to have a voice in or control over his learning.

Rules for talk and rules for silence vary across individuals and cultures and have changed over time (e.g., Basso, 1990; Bock, 1976; Constable, 2005). The rules that guide the amounts and timing of silence and talk are always interrelated. Classrooms have both implicit and stated rules about talk and silence, even when they are not designated or labeled as such. For instance, Ms. Davis posted the following rules in her classroom:

> We come to school to learn.
> Respect yourself, your classmates, and your friends.
> Walk quietly in the classroom, hallway, and stairs.
> Be patient, prepared, and persistent.
> Always try your best!

Ms. Davis's rules reflect the value she placed on respect in her classroom. She insisted that students show respect for themselves and for others. She taught them about this value and other values that were important to her through personal stories, her own actions, and by holding high expectations for the students. For instance, she wanted the students to value helping one another rather than always turning to their teachers or other adults. In order to explain and emphasize the importance of this practice, she told them a story about herself as a first grader. As a child, she could read but could not tie her own shoes. When her shoelaces were untied, her classmates knew to help her until she learned how to tie them on her own. In turn, she helped her classmates learn to read. By creating a set of classroom rules and norms and explaining them through stories, Ms. Davis urged her students to draw on their own strengths in order to help one another through talk and silence. Their education was both an individual and a collective goal.

In particular contexts and times, and for particular people, there are explicit and sometimes unstated rules for who can speak, and the timing, content, and form of their speech. These rules govern class participation. In most classrooms, there are rules that students should remain silent when the teacher or a peer has the floor. A student might apply this rule to instances when a teacher asks a rhetorical question (Mehan, 1979). As a result, a student's silent response to the teacher's question might reflect that the student knows the answer and understands that the teacher knows the answer as well. Accordingly, for that student, there is no need to state the answer out loud. Students might follow or, alternatively, decide to break the norms for speech and silence in a classroom. They might also invent their own rules for when they can or should participate. Like talk, silence is patterned in culturally specific ways that vary according to geography and tradition as much as categories such as race, class, and gender (Basso, 1990; Braithwaite, 1985). There might be family or community norms for behavior that students bring into the classrooms. Basso (e.g., 1979) would claim that these decisions are not based solely on cultural norms but also on relationships. In a classroom, these relationships include those between and among teachers and students. These rules are not inviolate and are likely to change in practice over time. Too often, a student who breaks a norm is perceived as resistant (or quiet), rather than as someone who is following a different set of rules or expectations.

The rules for how and when to enact silence and talk vary according to the function of the silence, the norms of the classroom space, and the traditions followed by different teachers and students (Bock, 1976). Ms. Davis introduced the activity in the above scene by using the familiar classroom routine—"Eyes on me"—to gather the students' attention. She concluded it by asking students to "give a thumbs up" or silent praise for each piece. She gave the initial command in an upbeat yet direct voice, and the students responded quickly. There are several common techniques that teachers use to enact a classroom norm to ask for or demand silence. Using another technique, Ms. Davis might have flicked the lights—an action that would have made the same statement with the same tone and likely would have elicited the same response. The silence she requested was one of respect for her and the students who would read their stories. Alternatively, she might have used another all-too-common technique and yelled, "Silence!", demanding attention and threatening punishment if her words were not heeded. This would have elicited the same response (silence), with a different tone. It would have been a different kind of silence—a silence of compliance rather than one of participation. Silence can be used to show praise, such as the silence Ms. Davis requested by modeling the convention of "thumbs up" for a job well done, or it can be used as a threat, such as the silent response of students to a teacher's loud voice or rebuke.

In responding to their classmate Terrell, students followed both the explicit rules and the implicit norms of the classroom. For instance, the students knew that even without the teacher's explicit permission, they could move closer to help their peers when they read their stories aloud to the class. As noted previously, Ms. Davis had a flexible set of rules that guided peers to assist one another. There was an expectation that students would use their peers as resources. At the beginning of the year, she informed the class that they would help one another and answer each other's questions, especially when she was teaching another group of students. Some teachers insist on total silence during work and writing periods. Ms. Davis encouraged students to turn to each other before coming to her. In order for this to occur, she taught them an explicit system. Her instructions in September were to begin with the number two: Students were told to ask two people their questions before coming to the teacher. If neither of those students could provide help, they were allowed to interrupt her. Later in the year, the number was increased to three, four, and then five. She gradually taught the students to rely on one another through structures that guided their interactions. This was reinforced by a classroom culture of respect and collaboration that they developed together over time. For instance, the first graders asked Terrell for help in finding lost objects, a particular strength of his. He, in turn, asked them for help with his reading and writing. By specifically pointing out and affirming each of the students' strengths in the course of a day, Ms. Davis assisted them in this process.

Without explicit instructions, the students generalized this rule or principle to other settings, maintaining the underlying value of respect by turning to one another for help and enacting a respectful silence when their peers spoke or read a story aloud. Through a balance of talk and silence, they embodied this value. In the scene above, when Terrell read his story with the silent assistance of his peers, a few students shifted their positions closer to him in order to help him when he seemed to be stuck. The negotiations for helping Terrell were completed in silence. The students moved and spoke in response to the immediate activity rather than to a prescribed rule established by the teacher. There were no explicit rules to guide this activity other than the basic ground rule, taught and lived by their teacher, of respect for one another and for themselves as learners. People have different ways of showing and enacting respect. In this classroom, the students learned from their teacher to show respect through silently guiding and encouraging their peers. The fact that their teacher silently sat with them in the circle as they listened to their peer read his story was a powerful enactment of this value. Her silent affirmation of the students taught them about silence.

The scene would have been dramatically different if the teacher had delivered orders or directions from the front of the class, a more typical classroom pattern of interaction. If Terrell's peers had called him names or acted meanly because he faltered, Ms. Davis would have had to intervene to maintain order and a respectful classroom climate. If she had worried that this might happen, she would have anticipated it and interrupted the students' movement toward Terrell when it began, insisting that it was his turn and his turn alone. By this point in the year, however, Ms. Davis was confident in the students' care for one another. As a result, she could guide the classroom interaction through silence. At the same time, the students knew one another well enough that they could negotiate turns for helping Terrell through silence. Rather than fighting for the privilege to help their classmate, as might be typical in another classroom, they moved in and out of that position, sharing the role. They enacted an implicit set of norms that Ms. Davis had taught them during the year through her own actions and stories of how she needed help as a child.

There are many different kinds of classroom rules for regulating silence and talk. The most common rule is insistence on silence while an individual—usually the teacher but sometimes the student—speaks. In classrooms, there are extended times for silence, such as during individual-work times, as well as times for student talk, such as during group-work times. When teachers change the norms (e.g., allowing talk during individual-work times or insisting on relative silence during group projects), they introduce new rules or reinforce existing ones. Students learn rules for talk and silence by paying attention to the stated rules and also by watching their teacher to learn the implicit ones. Ms. Davis's interactions with students were primarily gentle and supportive, and the students learned to imitate her actions, affirming one another through silence as well as talk.

Teachers and students use silence in a wide range of ways that reflect their understandings of classroom norms. In her study of classroom interactions in majority-Black urban classrooms, Gilmore (1983, 1985) offers an analysis of how students use silence in what she calls "silent displays." She recounts two examples of teachers whose reprimands were met by student silence. In the first instance, the teacher interpreted the silence as acquiescence, in the second, as resistance. The first enactment of silence was deemed acceptable by the teacher, who was able to retain her authority because she interpreted the student's silence as a sign of respect, apology, and remorse. In the second instance, however, the teacher interpreted the student's silence as an act of defiance, and the child was sent to the office. Gilmore (1985) labeled this defiant response, signaled by the child's nonverbal expressions, as "stylized sulking" or silence displays that students used in order to save face in front of their peers when they were in a direct confrontation with an adult in a position of authority. These interactions illustrate the unspoken norms that guided the rules for silence and response.

Moreover, Gilmore's observations revealed that Black teachers were more likely to respond more harshly to the "stylized sulking" of Black students than their White colleagues, who tended to ignore or tolerate the behavior. However, the "stylized sulking" led the White teachers to categorize students who enacted this behavior as failures. Rather than administering direct consequences to the children as a result of their behavior, such as sending the student to the office, the teachers enacted a response that had far-reaching academic consequences that they never directly communicated or acknowledged. In other words, there were no explicit rules stating that students should not sulk or respond with nonverbal facial expressions or stances; however, students who did not follow the implicit rules paid a high price through acquiring reputations as defiant and failing students.

Students and teachers bring their own implicit and explicit rules that guide behavior in the classroom. Most often, these are learned in families, communities, religious institutions, and the media. They are also learned in schools, from the first day in the classroom. There are circulating norms and rules that implicitly guide classroom interactions. Rules learned at home or in the community might align well with the classroom rules or, conversely, students may have to adapt to unfamiliar rules. For instance, students who are the only children in their families may have to learn to live and work with others at school. Teachers' rules are generally connected to a focus on academics and achievement and, by necessity, are often designed to control large groups of students to maintain order. This can be done explicitly through stating rules up front—which most teachers do—and also implicitly through guiding behavior and issuing consequences. Teachers establish rules to regulate talk and silence in their classrooms, and they also model rules through their own speech and silence. When Ms. Davis guided the interactions around Terrell's reading through silence, she modeled a set of implicit rules about respect for students, protecting their authority for their own texts. When students negotiated turns for helping Terrell in silence, they followed Ms. Davis's lead, respecting one another, and keeping the attention on Terrell rather than on themselves.

It would be difficult for a teacher to learn all of the rules that each child brings to the school, and these rules may or may not be relevant to the smooth running of classrooms. However, it is critical for teachers to be aware of when and how they might have rules that are different from those to which a student is accustomed, in order to learn how to change the rules to be more responsive to all students, accommodate individual students, or explicitly teach students the norms of the classroom. This stance of listening deeply to students is critical for democratic practice (Schultz, 2003). If classrooms are built on ideas of respect and participation, then teachers are better able to ensure that each student has a fair chance to participate and be heard through either talk or silence. Although including silence as a form of participation will not by itself lead to more democratic classrooms, it may allow teachers to move closer to this ideal.

Culturally responsive teaching (e.g., Gay, 2000; Ladson-Billings, 1994; Nieto, 2000) suggests that teachers build classroom norms around respect for the dispositions, knowledge, skills, and experiences students bring to school. This is even more complicated in many contemporary classrooms that have students from a wide diversity of cultural backgrounds. I suggest that in all classrooms, whether diverse or not, paying careful attention to the rules for talk and silence can lead teachers and students to more engaged and inclusive classroom practices.

Structuring Talk, Structuring Silence

A closer examination of a portion of the transcript from the above scene when Terrell read his story from the Author's Chair illustrates how both silence and talk played a role in structuring the event. In Figure 3.1, the role of silence in this scene is apparent. (See the Appendix for an explanation of the notations and a more complete transcript; see also Howard, 2006; Schultz, 2006a.)

After he settled in the Author's Chair, Terrell focused his attention on his teacher for cues about how to proceed. He looked to his teacher before he began to read. Once he started to read, however, he turned for help to his peers who were sitting close to him. There was a clear feeling of trust when he looked to Taisha and then Dillon for help in reading the words he had written. In response, Dillon scooted on his knees over to Terrell. After receiving help from Dillon, Terrell reclaimed his authorship, reorienting himself to the book. This entire transaction occurred in silence. From her position as a member of the group, Ms. Davis monitored the scene, creating a space from which Terrell could negotiate and receive help from his peers through an exchange of very few words. The only spoken words were those offered by the students who helped Terrell proceed with his performance. And even those words were spoken very softly, keeping

Figure 3.1. Transcript with white space to represent silence

---

 1 *Terrell*   [*(opens booklet to first page, flashes his eyes over to*
             right, carefully folds back front cover, flashes his eyes
             to the left, keeps folding, then flashes his eyes to the right
             again, looks down at page)
 2 Terrell   **I:,**
 3
 4
 5
 6
 7   **want   to: be: ay**
 8
 9   **[better: [([writer**
10
11 *Terrell*   [*(looks at Ms. Davis,* [*looks at page,* [*looks at Ms. Davis)*
12 Terrell   **I:,   want**
13
14
15   **to:**
16
17
18
19
20 *Terrell*   [*((looking intently at the page)*
21 Taisha   **((*quietly*))** [(   )
22 *Terrell*   [*(looks at Taisha*
23 Dillon   **((*quietly*)) [(I know/mmm) (I'm trying to) help him**
24 *Terrell*   [*(looks at Dillon as he approaches*
25 *Dillon*   [*(walks on knees up to Terrell's chair, grabs paper (Terrell still holds it),*
                 turns it toward himself and looks at the page)
26 Dillon   **((*quietly*)) ruh-   [writer,**
27 *Dillon*   [*(looking at Terrell)*
28 Terrell   **writer:,**
29
30
31
32
33
34   [*(Terrell pulls booklet out of Dillon's hands, looks down at page)*
35
36
37
38
39
40
41
42
43
44
45 Terrell   [[*glances at several students...*

Terrell at the center of the performance. Silence played a vital role in the teaching and learning activities in this scene.

Ms. Davis introduced several kinds of participation structures into her classroom. In addition to the Author's Chair, there were other structures, such as Chit Chat, Check In, and Reflections at the end of the day, all described in detail below. Some of these structures, like the Author's Chair, reflected Ms. Davis's beliefs about teaching in a manner that includes student voice in the classroom. Others, like Guided Reading Groups (e.g., Fountas & Pinnell, 1996), reflected the mandates of the school district. Classroom participation structures focus on turn-taking, roles and responsibilities, and the relationship between talk and silence. They are guided by rules, which determine speaking rights. For instance, in small-group structures, students can nominate themselves to speak. For the groups introduced by Ms. Davis, students had prescribed roles that they learned and practiced at the beginning of the year. Each year, Ms. Davis adapted common structures like the Author's Chair to the particular context of her classroom.

One way to analyze the interactions during the Author's Chair event is to focus on the speakers and listeners as well as the allocation of speaking rights. An examination of the role of silence in the above transcript highlights Ms. Davis's silence as Terrell negotiated the text, the long periods of Terrell's silence as he struggled to read each word, and the relatively silent negotiations enacted by the students as they came to Terrell's assistance. Paying attention to the spaces between the words that were said aloud, so that the silence rather than the talk is in focus, opens up new ways for teachers to attend to student learning.

By holding onto silence as she observed and guided the interactions, Ms. Davis allowed Terrell to retain control of his learning by giving him authority in the moment. Terrell's silence indicated his need for help to read his text aloud. His glance toward his teacher and later toward his classmates indicated his desire for their support and his nomination of them to come to his assistance. Rather than instructing students to help him, Ms. Davis established a context for the students to initiate and orchestrate this assistance on their own. This series of interactions takes on new meanings when read through the silence. In this instance, Terrell used silence to add time to his performance, which allowed him the space to think through and decipher the words on the page.

In Chapter 1, I introduced the concept of participation structure, which highlights the organizational structures that allow for (and inhibit) particular kinds of interactions (cf., Philips, 1972). This construct highlights how the actions of the students and teacher, whether verbal or silent, contribute to Terrell's performance. In order to understand an exchange, it is essential to take into account the whole constellation of speakers and hearers rather than to focus on single utterances by individuals. Terrell's performance can be understood in relation to the norms and expectations of the classroom that were enacted by his teacher and peers. Like most students, Terrell began reading by aligning himself with his teacher. He looked at her when he read the initial page of his book. She responded with silent encouragement without moving or speaking aloud. In the midst of his second page—and the second sentence—Taisha made a bid to help him by quietly speaking. In response, Terrell realigned himself in relation to his peers, looking to Taisha and later to Dillon as he worked to read the next few pages. Noticing this shift illuminates what happened through positioning and interaction as well as through the actual words that were said aloud.

In this interaction, there was significantly more silence than talk. It is unusual to see this much silence in a classroom, without a teacher stepping in to move things forward. In effect, the silence structured the talk and gave it meaning. Silence in classrooms, except when it indicates compliance and student attention, is usually viewed as negative. As explained previously, in the early studies of American Indian classrooms (e.g., Dumont, 1972; Erickson & Mohatt, 1982; Philips, 1972), teachers' and researchers' goals were to understand silence and then change classrooms, shifting participation structures to increase talk and eliminate silence. The perceived problem of these classrooms was that students were too silent (for a critique and exploration of this, see Foley, 1995, 1996; Lomawaima & McCarty, 2006; McCarty et al., 1991). The scene in Ms. Davis's classroom demonstrates that silence can be productive, giving students authority over their work and the work of their peers, and reframing individual performances as collective enterprises.

As introduced in Chapter 1, Cage's (1961) composition "4'33" illustrates that distinguishing music from silence is a matter of framing. Silence occurs, Cage suggests, when we shift our focus away from sounds. In the absence of music, the ambient sounds—generally considered a component of silence—are reframed as sound and part of the musical composition. In classroom talk and music, then, the framing or structure of an event can point to the salience of silence. The construct of framing determines how we understand a participant's verbal participation or nonverbal cues, such as a nod, as participation. Framing also affects whether ambient noise is counted as silence or music. In Cage's piece, the ambient noises—the coughs and shuffling of the audience—become the musical composition. In the classroom, the silent response or movement of a student takes on meaning in particular contexts and can be counted as participation. Learning can be located in the pauses between Terrell's words and the movement of the students as they crawl on their knees to assist him. This understanding is only apparent if we shift our focus from talk to silence. Shifting figure and ground, moving from talk to silence, our reading of classroom interaction changes.

A focus on the role of silence illuminates the flow of power between and among the teacher and students in this scene, pointing to the new forms of learning and social interaction that transpire in the silence as well as the talk. Attention to the distribution of power and control is central to the conceptualization of democratic practice. In addition, the analysis of silence points to new forms of knowledge and the ways knowledge circulates through both talk and silence in the classroom. Terrell's performance could easily be read as that of a first-grade student who is working below grade level, struggling to write and subsequently barely able to read the few sentences he wrote. With such a focus, his failure, rather than the success of the group, would be the story. Alternatively, the notion of participation frameworks within situated contexts focuses our attention on the social accomplishment of this literacy event, highlighting the collaborative efforts of the group to read the written text within the classroom context at this particular moment. Within this frame, through collaborative efforts, Terrell's success becomes the story.

McDermott (cf., 1974, 1987, 1988; Varenne & McDermott, 1999) has argued persuasively over the years that opportunities for participation shape possibilities for learning. Beginning with high and low reading groups and extending his analysis to sites such as adult literacy programs, afterschool clubs, and classroom contexts, he has carefully traced how schools, through norms of behavior and rules for participation, are systematically organized to produce failure. In his terms, failure acquires people, rather than the other way around. He raises questions about whether participation structures need to be adapted to the home and community cultures of school children, as suggested by research in the 1970s and 1980s, or whether educators need to focus instead on the ways in which success is predicated on failure.

At the end of Terrell's first-grade year, he struggled to read the very few words he put on his page. Although Ms. Davis knew of his accomplishments outside of school and in a few other classroom activities, if he had been asked to read his story aloud without the support of his classmates and teacher, he would have been set up to fail (interview, 4/5/08). Educators have choices to make about how they organize their classrooms. Many of these decisions lead to the success and failure of students. A focus on the silence of the students and their teacher in this scene allows us to see how this participation structure, with opportunities for Terrell to read in collaboration with his peers, allowed him to join in a classroom routine as the author of his text. Although he may have been a failing student (and did, in fact, repeat a grade), in this moment, he could be said to have successfully performed the school task by reading his story aloud to the class. Making silence visible shifts the focus away from a single student struggling alone with a text, reframing his performance as a collective accomplishment.

An analysis of silence illustrates how Terrell was able to perform as a successful student in this moment, even though he frequently struggled to complete reading and writing tasks throughout the year. In this moment and others like it, his performance can be understood by paying attention to the silence that surrounded the talk and situated activity. Over time, this kind of success could lead to more permanent changes in his relationship to academic pursuits. The larger context of the classroom and, more broadly, the society or lifeworlds that these students and their teacher inhabit shape the possibilities for learning for Terrell. Understanding how silence works in the classroom illuminates this process and can inform teaching.

The construct of participation structures and the attendant analyses of power relations are useful for understanding the relationships between silence and talk in the Author's Chair event. Rather than enforcing student silence, the classroom structure, including the allocation of speaking rights and turn-taking (cf., Au & Jordan, 1981; Cazden, 2001; Hymes, 1964), allowed for teacher and student silence that supported student "success." In this instance, silence, rather than talk, structured the interactions between teachers and students. The teacher shared power with the students by allowing them to initiate turns and author their actions. As a result, the students undoubtedly felt more confident about themselves, at least in the moment. Teachers may feel uneasy about remaining silent in their classrooms, assuming that by doing so, they are not actively teaching. Just as students can actively participate in classrooms through silence, teachers can take an active role in teaching through remaining silent, yet attentive, as Ms. Davis illustrates. Teachers' silence reframes students' understanding of their own silence and participation. Key to these teacher decisions is whether the silence is opening up or closing down participation. Just as the silence can allow others to talk and take authority, a person's silence can silence others.

Ms. Davis's use of silence was predicated on trust and a willingness to share power and authority. She trusted the students to be kind to Terrell and to act respectfully toward him as he struggled to read aloud. Terrell, in turn, trusted that his classmates would help him through his reading, rather than teasing him. As a result, he agreed to read his story aloud and also to accept help from his peers. This was no small accomplishment. An exploration of trust is critical for understanding silence as participation. When teachers tightly control student interaction, they convey little trust to their students for initiating their own learning and engagement. Ms. Davis struck a balance. She intentionally and slowly built trust with her students over the course of the year. She did not naively or blindly trust her students and expect that they would automatically trust her and one another; rather, they all worked together to develop routines and inter-actions that reflected this belief. This trust was laced with the talk and si-lence through which Ms. Davis taught.

SILENCE AND CLASSROOM ROUTINES

Teachers instruct with silence by adding silence to their classrooms, and when necessary, breaking that silence. The concept of "wait time" (Rowe, 1986) describes how teachers add silence to their classrooms in order to encourage otherwise quiet students to speak. Teachers can create silence or spaces in their classrooms in order to invite talk from students who are easily overlooked or unheard. A common technique taught to new teachers is to count to five or ten before calling on a student, ensuring that students who take a longer time to formulate responses have an opportunity to participate. Another strategy is to ask a question with multiple possible responses (e.g., descriptive phrases), and then give each child an oppor-tunity to add to the conversation. Providing the time, structure, and ex-pectation for each student to make a contribution to a class discussion and guaranteeing silence when the student speaks may encourage some stu-dents to speak who may otherwise remain silent. In addition, there are times when students may need to participate through silence, and educa-tors can find ways to adapt classroom structures and develop an ability to understand this form of participation. At the same time, there are times when it may be necessary for a teacher to insist on verbal contributions from students. Certain conversations may depend on vocal participation from each member of the class. A teacher may need to hear a student's response out loud in order to gauge learning. Pushing a student to articu-late an idea out loud may reinforce a critical skill or disposition to learn-ing. One way to do this is by adding silence to classrooms.

Adding Silence

Ms. Davis had a routine in her classroom called "Check In." She brought the students into a circle on the rug for a "Check In" for a variety of rea-sons, including the desire to respond to an event that disturbed the rhythm of the classroom, to rebuild community when there were bad feelings among the students, or simply to gather the class together as a group in order to refocus the students' attention. The following vignette illustrates one such moment.

> The children were seated in a circle with their journals in their laps. Like any group of first graders, they were wiggling around. Ms. Davis explained to the class, "We need a Check In," and instructed them to put down their journals. Students echoed her words "check in" and began to recite the formal phrase that opened the routine. Ms. Davis quieted them, letting them know that Check In had not yet begun and that one of the students would be the leader. Once this was established, Ms. Davis nodded to the student leader and joined him in repeating the opening phrase of "Check In." Before they finished the second word, the rest of the children chimed in: "The circle cannot be broken. Put our feelings on the table. Let them flow." Ms. Davis carefully explained the protocol, which was familiar to each child. They were allowed to say anything except something about another person. They would start with one student and end with Ms. Davis. They each had about 20 seconds to speak. As she finished the explanation, Ms. Davis asked the class to repeat the phrase she had taught them if they chose not to speak: "I graciously decline."
>
> The appointed student started the Check In and, one by one, the other students followed, adding their feelings about the morning or the work they had accomplished. Some students had few words to contribute. Many repeated the phrase, "I graciously decline." Ms. Davis did not call on students or comment on their contributions. Without speaking, she nodded when they spoke, acknowledging their contributions, and then nodded to the next person to continue. At one point, a girl said nothing, shaking her head. Ms. Davis broke her own silence and prompted the student, "Say whatever you want or 'I graciously decline.'" When it was Ms. Davis's turn to speak, she talked about the morning:
>
>> I want to say, there were a lot of changes in here this morning and everyone really—considering—handled themselves quite well. I just need us to remember we are a group [the children joined in on the word *group*] and must work together. Even when people sometimes get on your last nerves. We must work together. Not work just for yourselves. Work with your classmates. We must always, we must always remember. The circle cannot be broken.

Administrators had come into her room that morning, disrupting
the work time to make her room neater and put curtains over
some of the closets to cover the clutter because of visitors. They
had told her sternly to get rid of the classroom pets (a rabbit and a
few birds), animals she had brought in to increase the home-like
feeling of her classroom. The administrators' presence in her
classroom had rattled her. She used the quiet moment to gather
the class together as a community so they could continue with
their academic routines.

After firmly telling a student to either join the circle or return
to his seat, Ms. Davis led the class in the final phase of the Check In
ritual. Together, they said, "The circle cannot be broken. Check In
is over. Let us go in peace. A 1-minute quiet reflection." Next, the
children sat together in silence squirming without saying a word
aloud. They concluded the ritual after the minute of silence with
an explanation from Ms. Davis that she was proud of the class.

Ms. Davis created several routines that included silent reflection. In
addition, with Check In, she set up a routine during which each child was
given the opportunity to speak or "graciously decline." Silence surrounded
the talk as children were encouraged to contribute to the discussion without judgment or evaluation. They were expected to listen to one another
in silence. The entire sequence took about 5 minutes and did not take a
significant amount of time away from the conventional instructional period. The payoff was substantial, as students were taught the value of silent reflection and of sitting together as a community in "a circle that
cannot be broken." Although the children were encouraged to speak, in
many ways, it was silence that bound the students and their teacher together in this brief event. Through the silence, they gathered together and
refocused on the work they needed to accomplish during the rest of the
day. This silent period was useful for the students and the teacher.

Ms. Davis instructed her students with silence. By remaining silent
during this Check In routine and during the Author's Chair, she allowed
students to take responsibility for their own learning and for their peers. In
effect, they became teachers as well as learners and the holders of important knowledge. Her silence enabled those interactions to transpire. In addition, the silence increased the sense of community in the classroom, which
taught the students the value of listening to and helping one another, as
well as thinking of themselves as a cohesive and caring group, or a circle
that could not be broken. In Ms. Davis's classroom, silence was a marker
for a respectful rather than a disinterested, disengaged, or resistant student.
She demonstrated this through her practices and daily actions.

Hori (1994) describes teaching and learning in a Zen monastery, a contemporary Buddhist temple in Japan. In this unique setting, teaching and learning are directly tied to practice rather than to the production of answers. The learning process is learner-initiated and always connected to the learner's need to know something. Teaching and learning occur through silence rather than through talk. As Hori explains, Zen monks are expected to learn without being taught, and the goal of the teaching is to produce a better (or more educated) person rather than to impart particular skills. Motivation for learning is tied directly to tasks that need to be learned and accomplished.

In Ms. Davis's class, students learned the value of talk and participation through joining in this 5-minute ritual of Check In time. They were taught the value of their own ideas and feelings and were provided room to express these freely rather than through prescribed responses to textbook questions. They were also reminded of the importance of community. Ms. Davis taught these values through enacting a ritual and through the repetition of several ritualistic phrases, such as "the circle cannot be broken." Children learned their responsibilities as members of a classroom community. The reflection time at the end gave them the space to absorb these ideas and make them their own. Charles Courtenay wrote the first treatise on silence, *The Empire of Silence*, in 1916. He posited that teachers who demanded silence will never attain it because they impose it from the outside rather than cultivating an internal capacity for remaining silent (cited in Clair, 1998). In her classroom, through brief routines, Ms. Davis gave students the opportunity to develop the capacity for silence and reflection. In Friends' schools, the practice of Quaker Meeting invites people to sit in silence together; participants speak out of the silence. This practice provides the same kind of opportunity for children to learn from and respond within silence as a part of daily classroom practice. Through sitting in silence, students learn about their inner resources, at the same time affirming their connection to the community.

In addition to reflective periods and wait time, teachers can add silence to their classrooms within talk, ensuring that there are pauses and spaces, or what Greene (1988) calls "openings" in the talk. She describes her conception of openings as both physical and metaphorical:

> Such efforts . . . unleash imagination in unexpected ways. They draw the mind to what lies beyond the accustomed boundaries and often to what is not yet. They do so as persons become more and more aware of the unanswered questions, the unexplored corners, the nameless faces behind forgotten windows. These are the obstacles to be transcended if understanding is to be gained. (p. 128)

Openings, according to Greene, include spaces in talk that are more than literal pauses. These openings contain possibilities and underscore what we do not and cannot know. The idea of creating openings suggests participation in a classroom through the stance of not knowing all the answers, of nurturing curiosity, and of leaving room for possibility. This stance necessarily includes silence.

Learning is compromised when classrooms are filled with teacher talk and exercises to produce expected answers. By creating openings for students to express themselves—for instance, in periods of silence, in writing imaginative narratives or research reports based on their own expertise, or in open-ended and personal responses to stories—teachers cultivate students' imaginations, open up forums for participation, and create more inclusive, democratic classrooms. Silence can provide children and their teachers with space for thinking and responding to immediate problems, deepening their thinking about long-term and more complex questions, and resisting facile solutions.

Ms. Davis had another routine that she enacted at the end of every day called "Reflections." At the beginning of the year, she simply had the children list all the activities they remembered from the day. She hoped that after this activity, they would be able to answer the question frequently posed by family members, "What did you do in school today?" She also wanted the children to see how much they had accomplished each day. After a few weeks, Ms. Davis made a T-chart or a chart with two columns, and wrote a question above each of the columns with room for responses: "What did we do?" and "What did we learn?" She instructed the students to use these same questions for their own reflections before a group conversation. Sometimes, she would ask them to write their own reflections in response to the questions before the group conversation. In the spring, she added a third column: "How did I learn it?" The first few times these questions were introduced, the students often responded with silence. Ms. Davis would let them sit in silence—sometimes for long periods of time—until they began to generate the lists of activities. In response to the silence, she would often say, "Let us think. It's okay to think." This taught them to be comfortable with silence and the space to think. As she explained, "Sometimes there were great moments of silence" (interview, 4/5/08). The periods of reflection and silence allowed the students to consolidate their learning and gain a better sense of their own knowledge.

Teachers rarely save time during the day for reflection. Responding to the pressure to raise test scores, teachers often feel obligated to fill every minute. Students who need moments of silence to extend their thinking and put their thoughts into words are often labeled "silent" or "slow." By adding silence to the classroom, Ms. Davis allowed the students and herself to slow down and see for themselves what they had learned each day. Check In and Reflections each took about 5 to 10 minutes from beginning to end. Yet, in these small amounts of time, punctuated by silence, students were able to develop the habit of reflection and build a sense of shared responsibility for learning.

Breaking Silence

In contrast to the productive silence described above, there are times when silence in classrooms indicates a lack of active participation and teachers may need to shift away from that silence, as illustrated in the following scene from Ms. Davis's classroom. There were times when simply adding silence was not enough to generate the kind of engaged dialogue that Ms. Davis desired and expected from her first graders.

> The students were gathered together in front of the teacher, who read from a biography of Helen Keller. When Ms. Davis reached the end of Chapter 1, she closed the book, and asked, "Think about what Helen must be going through and how Helen must be feeling, how the parents must be feeling." Her rising intonation indicated that this was a question. Most students responded with silence. A few students ventured one-word responses, such as "sad" and "crying." These responses to how Helen and her parents were feeling at this critical moment in the story, after Helen had just displayed a fit of anger, did not satisfy Ms. Davis, who knew that the students had more to say than their single-word responses. After a few minutes, she issued these directions: "At this time, I would like to have a Chit Chat. I would like everyone to stand. . . . Please get into a small group of children that you do not mind speaking with, but do not speak with them yet. . . . Make a circle with whomever you are with."
> Without further directions or talk, the students stood up, arranging themselves into small clusters. Ms. Davis signaled them to begin speaking with one another in their small groups. She did not explicitly give instructions about how they should organize this talk, although previously they had practiced having a Chit Chat many times. The classroom was immediately filled with noise. In stark contrast to the single-word responses, the students offered more elaborate answers in conversation with their friends. Each group moved in closer to hear the other members of the group; several clusters of children, arms around one another in huddles, excitedly talked about the book.

After several minutes, Ms. Davis was satisfied and instructed
the students to come back together as a group. Rather than asking
them to repeat their conversations—a routine that is typical,
especially with older students—she moved on to the next topic.

In switching the classroom routine to a Chit Chat, Ms. Davis's goal
had been to check the students' comprehension and to make sure that they
attended to the details of the Helen Keller story. She was satisfied with
their responses and made a decision to continue with her teaching. This
decision, among others, is instructive to teachers who think they need to
hear learning in order for it to count.

When students responded to Ms. Davis's initial question with relative silence, she made the choice to break the silence and shift the participation structure. She did this by asking the students to move into small
groups to join in conversations that they initiated themselves. In many of
the groups, a single child repeated the question—"How did Helen feel?"—
to prompt the conversations. By shifting to smaller, more intimate contexts for participation, Ms. Davis was able to move the class from silence
to talk. Rather than reprimanding the students for their lack of participation or deciding to revise the question, Ms. Davis made structural changes
to the classroom dynamic, introducing a new participation structure. Along
with these changes came different turn-taking rules and speaking rights.
In the whole-group discussion, the usual rules for talk and silence pre-
vailed. One person spoke at a time, while everyone else was silent. Although this is the typical pattern of interaction in classrooms, often it is
not conducive to engaged talk about text. By prompting students to physically shift their positions into smaller groups for just 3 minutes, Ms. Davis
was able change the pattern of who initiated and who participated in the
talk. Instead of silence and single-word responses, the young students participated in extended and more thoughtful conversations. In the Chit Chat
groups, the rules shifted so that anyone could offer a response without
waiting for the teacher's sanction and then listening for her evaluation.
Ms. Davis moved the class from an unproductive period of silence to a
productive period of talk. Further, students were given opportunities to
join the conversation without the pressure of speaking in front of the whole
class, a situation explored further in Chapter 4.

At the beginning of the year, Ms. Davis introduced a variety of participation structures to the students. Some of these were part of the regular routines of the classroom. Later, she introduced new routines as they
were needed. The Author's Chair was a central part of Ms. Davis's curriculum. In contrast, the Chit Chat groups arose more spontaneously out
of a need for smaller groups that allowed for greater participation. None-

theless, Ms. Davis carefully instructed the students on how to participate in a Chit Chat, scaffolding their learning. For the Chit Chat, each
group developed its own set of speaking rights and responsibilities, including rules for silence, which shifted each time new groups were formed
by the teacher. The students learned how to do this at the beginning of
the year by practicing with simple topics and clear instructions about how
and when to speak and listen. Before long, they could almost spontaneously form the groups, establish norms, and orchestrate conversations,
a notable accomplishment for children this young. Clear rules and norms
of respect guided their interactions with one another; their comfort with
silence and talk was clear.

Rules for silence are not simply the opposite of rules for speaking (e.g.,
a person should remain silent when another person is speaking). In the
smaller Chit Chat groups, students were still expected to remain quiet while
another student spoke, but there could be (and was) more overlapping
speech. Students were not required to speak—there was no teacher directly monitoring their actions—however, they were expected to contribute as group members. As a result, most children participated through
speaking; others contributed through silence. A student who did not pay
attention while Ms. Davis read the story may have remained silent in
these small groups. Yet, he may have also found more reason to listen
because of his accountability to his peers, learning more about the story
in a context where it was safer not to have immediate answers. To ask a
question in a small group is likely to feel less risky or threatening than
raising the same question to the whole class. When students are held
accountable to their peers in addition to their teacher, their internal rules
for when to speak and when to remain silent may change. A student who
is not interested—or brave—enough to speak up in front of the whole class
may find more opportunities to speak in a more intimate setting. Teachers are often faced with silent classes. Ms. Davis's spontaneous decision to
shift the participation structures is instructive for these situations.

Ladson-Billings (1996) writes about how silence can be used by students at the university level to retreat from class and as a weapon against
their teacher. In addition, as a form of resistance, student silence can shift
a dialogic classroom into one that is dominated by teacher talk. Ladson-
Billings explores the dynamics of a class when White students refused
to speak in a class taught by a Black professor. Rather than labeling students as resistant, Ladson-Billings suggests that teachers ask themselves
about their own role in creating these silences. In other words, the introduction of talk and silence is the responsibility of both the instructor
and the students. The opportunities and spaces for talk and silence are
created by them both.

By changing norms for participation and silence, I suggest that teachers can shift dynamics in classrooms. Rather than a focus on the dynamic of teachers silencing students (or students' self-silencing), I argue that teachers can interrogate how silence works in classrooms and analyze the norms for silence and talk, an idea I elaborate in Chapter 5. For instance, in the classrooms described by Ladson-Billings, students' norms for silence and talk may vary according to their race, culture, class, and gender, and within and across those categories. These norms are always socially constructed in conjunction with teachers and reflective of norms in the local context at a specific moment in time, even if they are implicit and never stated aloud. An exploration of these norms with students may bring questions, decisions, and tensions to the surface in such a way that they can be safely discussed.

Tateishi (2007/2008), a Japanese American, writes about her noisy dinner table as a child, which contrasted sharply with the meals and conversational patterns of her Japanese American peers. Her father explicitly changed the rules from silence to talk at home to encourage his children to succeed in White American classrooms that expected talk rather than silence from the students. After the internment of American citizens of Japanese descent, he believed that it was important for his family, and especially his children, to learn to speak up. This shift in family norms had its desired effect.

As an educator and researcher interested in the education of Asian American students, among other topics, Tateishi was invited into a colleague's high school classroom to understand the silence of the Asian American students. After talking with and interviewing a group of students, Tateishi learned that it was useful to divide students into small groups to encourage talk. In addition, it was important to establish specific rules for speech—and presumably for silence—and a leader to regulate talk when the students were in small groups. This suggestion for the organization of groups is different from the Chit Chat groups that Mattie Davis set up, which did not have group leaders. All the same, the Chit Chat groups followed guidelines that Ms. Davis had taught the young students through practice at the beginning of the year. These examples suggest that the rules and structures that encourage talk in classroom settings are highly contextual. This range of solutions to perceived silence both reflect and shift classroom and group norms.

CONCLUSION: CONNECTING SILENCE TO LEARNING

There are many kinds of classrooms in the United States and around the world. There are classrooms dominated by teacher-initiated talk and student silence. Alternatively, there are classrooms filled with the noise of disruptive students that teachers are unable to silence and control. There are also noisy classrooms that contain focused students engaged in individual and group tasks that require talk among peers. These same classrooms might also have periods of silence when children read their own books during a time known as Sustained Silent Reading (SSR) or work silently on their own writing or school projects. The major difference between these varied classrooms is not whether they are quiet or noisy—although that quality might draw the attention of the outsider looking in—but whether the relative amount of silence or talk is intentional or controlled. Rather than advocating for any particular kind of classroom, this chapter argues that a focus on silence illuminates how teaching and learning occur in classrooms through both silence and talk and provides a way to broaden conceptions of who participates in classrooms, what that participation looks like, and how students participate.

Along with the increased emphasis on scripted curriculum, especially in urban areas and hard-to-staff schools in the United States, in the late 1990s and early part of the 21st century, there has been a renewed focus on direct instruction, in which the teacher stands at the front of the room and reads or adapts a script. Advocates of this pedagogical practice claim that this manner of teaching ensures that students have uniform and predictable experiences. The focus is on the words teachers say (or read) and the scripted verbal responses that students are expected to produce. Years ago, Goodlad (1984) found that teacher talk, used to control students' behavior and the content of their talk, dominated classrooms (cf., Cazden, 2001). As a result, researchers found that secondary students depend on this teacher talk rather than their own analysis and that of their peers when they read texts (Alvermann, O'Brien, & Dillon, 1990). Almost 2 decades later, these conditions persist in school. A focus on teacher talk as the dominant medium of instruction ignores the opportunities for both teaching and learning in and through silence. An analysis of the role of silence in classroom teaching provides new possibilities for pedagogical practice and a new lens for understanding classroom interactions. Many teachers understand the importance of breaking students into small groups to vary the patterns of participation in classrooms. In the context of rethinking and developing new understandings of participation, an analysis of silence in classroom discourse suggests new roles for teachers and students.

Most teachers seek to include all students in learning, shaping their practices to reach the range of students in their classrooms. A common practice is differentiated instruction in which teachers develop parallel activities to involve all students using materials tailored to the particular knowledge, skills, and needs of each group (e.g., Tomlinson, 1999). In order to match instruction to the students, content is varied to increase their participation. I suggest that in addition to focusing on content to draw in more students, it is critical to examine pedagogical practice (Schultz, 2003) and notice how students participate and teachers teach through both talk and silence. Shifting pedagogical practice to include more students holds promise for the creation of equitable classrooms that value and recognize all students' contributions.

The analysis of talk and silence in Ms. Davis's classrooms as well as classrooms more generally prompts questions such as:

- Who is allowed and even encouraged to participate, and who is excluded from participation in classrooms?
- How are classrooms structured to privilege certain kinds of participation to the exclusion of other forms of engagement?
- How are these rules connected to equity and access?
- What are the affordances and constraints for participation in the current climate of mandated curriculum and high-stakes testing?
- How are the rules for participation learned and taught?
- Finally, what counts as participation that adds or extends students' understandings, and what forms of participation are ignored, viewed as disruptive, or framed as "off topic"?

The next chapter extends this analysis through a discussion of curricular silences, raising similar questions in terms of students' silence and participation in relationship to curriculum, through an in-depth study of Amelia Coleman's fifth-grade classroom.

CHAPTER 4

Student Silences, Curricular Participation

IN ORDER TO build community and articulate her expectations for students on the first day of school, Amelia Coleman explained that the central norm of her fifth-grade classroom was respect. After a brief introductory activity, she asked the students to write about what respect looks like. When she asked what respect might *sound* like, Robin replied, "Silence." At first, Ms. Coleman said, "Sometimes it sounds like silence," and continued to solicit more answers.

A few turns later, Ms. Coleman decided to return to this idea of silence and elaborated her position on silence as a sign of respect:

> Sometimes it sounds like silence. Sometimes it sounds like kids thinking out loud. Sometimes if you respect your learning, you know it's okay to share. Share what's inside your brain. So sharing thoughts. Can we ask questions in our learning community? Should it sound like people asking questions? *If you're not talking, you're not learning.* If you're not asking questions, sharing your thoughts. It's not always a good thing to be silent all of the time. Asking questions, sharing thoughts. (field notes, 9/6/05; emphasis mine)

Ms. Coleman used Robin's suggestion that respect sounds like silence to emphasize her belief that learning occurs through talk rather than silence. Like many teachers, Ms. Coleman valued verbal participation, understanding it as a proxy for learning. She communicated these values to her students on the first day so that they would know what was expected of them in this classroom.

In this introductory lesson, Ms. Coleman reinforced the notion that student voice is a critical component of her pedagogical practice. (For a review of the literature on student voice, see Cook-Sather, 2002, 2006.) For many teachers, verbal participation in a classroom discussion indicates active engagement and learning. The act of making verbal contributions to a discussion suggests that a student is working to understand a concept and willing to put those thoughts into the public arena. In contrast, it is

83

commonly thought that silence represents withdrawal, disengagement, and a lack of participation. In this chapter, and throughout the book, I argue that, in addition to talk, it is critical for teachers to attend to silent participation for evidence of student learning. This chapter presents alternative practices to respond to this silence. In classrooms where silence as a form of participation is not acceptable or desirable, I suggest that teachers introduce new modes of participation, such as visual or multimodal projects. Through a discussion of a 4-year research project in Ms. Coleman's classroom, I explain how students who were previously marked as silent and perhaps disengaged gained a new position in the classroom as participatory students through their involvement in a curriculum based on multimodalities.

Our research in Amelia Coleman's classroom occurred at a time when high-stakes tests were used as the primary metric for learning in the United States. While individual teachers, especially those prepared in research-based teacher education programs, pay particular attention to student talk to gauge their learning, policymakers often view talk as subjective and difficult to evaluate. As a result, standardized tests have been developed to assess students' learning. The pressure exerted by these tests, especially through federal legislation in the United States such as the No Child Left Behind (NCLB) Act of 2001, drives curricular decisions, leading teachers to change their pedagogical practices and making it difficult to find the time to listen to and come to know students. In schools across the United States and much of the world, time is spent drilling students to prepare them to attain higher scores on these tests rather than connecting learning to their interests, passions, and knowledge. Although these practices may result in higher scores, it is not clear that they also result in deep and sustained learning. It is likely that students have fewer opportunities for active participation in classrooms constrained by standardized curriculum and a drive to improve test scores.

In this chapter, I show how adding multimodalities to a classroom is one way that a teacher can provide opportunities for all students to participate in classroom learning, expanding the opportunities beyond a reliance on written and verbal assessment. A goal of this chapter is to elaborate new indicators of student learning and participation that go beyond a focus on tests and student talk through a detailed description of one curricular project that included the integration of multimedia and multiple modalities. The project, which we call multimodal storytelling, allowed students to display their learning through participation that is visible as well as vocal. As she explained in the opening vignette, Amelia Coleman created a classroom community that used talk to connect students' lives to the curriculum. In this classroom, students who were silent were not considered to be fully engaged in learning; multimodal storytelling provided an alternative mode of participation. Through the creation and display of multimodal stories, students who were previously thought of as "silent" were able to become "good" students. In Chapter 1, I defined participation as verbal and nonverbal contributions to ongoing classroom interactions. Participation can be in an aural (spoken), visual (pictoral), or written (textual) form; students can also participate through silence. A focus on democratic participation highlights the salience of inclusive classroom environments that draw on multiple perspectives and sources of knowledge expressed through both talk and silence. This chapter elaborates a curricular activity that attempted to provide a range of ways for a variety of students to participate in school learning and a means for teachers to document and assess learning beyond tests and listening for student talk.

In a classroom that includes multimodalities, like Ms. Coleman's fifth grade, there are many ways for students to participate. Over the 4 years of the research project, we noticed that students who were often silent in this classroom were able to take on new roles and attain a more visible participatory presence in the classroom. I use the term *participatory presence* to indicate ways that students become engaged with their peers and the content of school learning so that their ideas enter the public domain, giving them a presence in the classroom community (see also Rodgers & Raider-Roth, 2006, for a discussion of presence). Participation in a community also includes learning from the ideas of others to collaboratively build a space where new thinking and perspectives can flourish. Students typically contribute to classroom discussions through talk. When students cannot find a way to enter into the classroom discourse through verbal modes, the introduction of multimodalities or alternative modes of participation allows them to join their peers and the teacher in learning. In this chapter, I explore how students participated through modes other than verbal communication and how a curriculum of multimodal storytelling—or a range of ways to compose and display stories—gave students new opportunities to bring their knowledge and stories into the classroom and to become marked as "good" or participatory students. Adding new modes for representation of ideas allowed more students to participate in classroom life.

Ms. Coleman emphasized that each of these forms of participation—listening, writing, and talk—was essential to learning in her classroom, making the classroom norms explicit by emphasizing her expectation that everyone would speak during classroom discussions. In contrast to an understanding of pedagogy as covering material or depositing knowledge in the minds of students, teachers like Ms. Coleman begin with what children know, understand, and are curious about as a basis for building knowledge together. Ms. Coleman's decision to form a learning community that values each child's contributions reflects a belief that curriculum and pedagogy are dynamic and intertwined. Curriculum is broader than the information in textbooks and includes knowledge brought to school by children and teachers and the pedagogical decisions made by a teacher in response to her students. Ms. Coleman's belief that each child's voice should be represented in classroom discussions is both a pedagogical and curricular decision. By adding multimodalities or more ways to participate in classrooms, the conceptions of voice, silence, and participation are expanded.

THE LIMITS OF MULTICULTURAL CURRICULUM AS A RESPONSE TO STUDENT SILENCES

In the United States and across the world, the demographics of public schools are changing, and in many instances, schools are becoming more diverse as a result of transnational immigration. Along with this increased diversity, youth have growing access to a wide array of popular culture and new media. Paradoxically, despite these opportunities for exposure to new ideas and perspectives, there has been a press for standardization and uniformity inside of schools. These trends towards uniformity in pedagogy and curriculum ignore the rapid changes in demography and the changing content of students' lives (Schultz, 2003; Schultz & Throop, in press). As schools adopt more standardized curricula and uniform pedagogical and linguistic practices, they risk losing influence in students' lives. With the proliferation of opportunities for youth to engage in learning and the exchange of ideas outside of schools, the narrowing of school curriculum has made the content of school learning less relevant and meaningful to youths' lives.

This chapter addresses the relationships between curricular openings and possibilities, participation, and silence in Amelia Coleman's classroom. Debates about the content and delivery of curriculum have been steady features of public education in the United States. Rarely do they incorporate discussions of participation. The debates hinge on conflicting understandings of the purposes of education and contested beliefs about which interest groups should be allowed to determine whose knowledge is most valuable (Apple, 1979, 2000; Kliebard, 1966), rather than how these ideas are taken up and responded to through talk and silence in the classroom. As Apple (2000) emphasizes, school knowledge is not neutral. What counts as legitimate school knowledge is a product of complex power relations and struggles among various groups of people with a vested interest in what is taught.

During the first part of the 20th century, the dominant purpose of public education in the United States was to assimilate immigrants into the so-called mainstream. The central function of schooling was to produce American citizens. The ideology of assimilation was not widely challenged until the 1950s and 1960s when there was an attempt to replace this model with a more pluralistic discourse that was translated into a wide variety of programs and curricular materials (McCarthy, 1993). In the 1970s, multicultural education emerged, in part, as a response to the failure of the compensatory policies of the Kennedy and Johnson administrations (cf., Banks, 1993b). A goal of the multicultural education movement was to create curricula that more accurately reflected and embodied the diversity of the United States, educating *all* students in the histories and cultures of the people who are residents of this country.

The topics addressed by specific curricula are highly contested, and their selection reflects basic assumptions about the purposes of schooling. They reflect whose knowledge and perspectives are valued and, conversely, whose history, knowledge, and understandings are devalued or erased. Curricular omissions often lead students to withdraw from participation in classrooms, establishing their own patterns of silence over time. In contrast, curricular openings invite students to connect new learning to what they already know, understand, and value (Greene, 1988; Remillard & Geist, 2002).

Scholars such as McCarthy (1988) critique multicultural education, claiming that its mainstream acceptance was a "curricular truce" (p. 267) that was designed to address the demands of various racial groups in the 1960s and 1970s. More recently, educators such as Ladson-Billings (2003) have argued that multicultural education must go beyond a focus on single groups to include multiple forms of difference and a global emphasis. Nieto (2000) urges educators to emphasize a focus on equity and student learning in multicultural education. These goals were central to Amelia Coleman's practice and visible in her curricular choices and interactions with students. For instance, in response to a question about why she chose a text about Paul Robeson, Ms. Coleman explained,

> I know they know about unfairness. I know they know what it means to be courageous and brave. [The book] tells about someone who looks a lot like them having to overcome challenges. They are going to have to make decisions to change the world . . . if I don't help them to make those connections. I think I will lose them." (interview, 6/6/06)

At the same time that Ms. Coleman found books for the students about people with whom they might identify, she acknowledged their struggles, giving them the skills and tools they needed to succeed beyond her classroom.

Although the multiculturalism movement has changed the content of curriculum from preschool through university education in most parts of the United States, it has rarely fundamentally altered pedagogical practices. In Ms. Coleman's classroom, there were many books and posters that reflected the diversity of the United States. In the standardized curriculum she was told to teach, there were texts that reflect cultural diversity for teachers to use. As Banks (e.g., 1993b) and others explain, a central goal of multicultural education is not only to teach the knowledge and perspectives of a wide variety of groups, including their ways of knowing, but also to convey strategies for critical analysis of this information. Although curriculum materials like the textbooks in Ms. Coleman's classroom have stories that represent a relatively wide range of ethnicities and experiences, they rarely address the central conflicts that characterize much of history (e.g., Apple, 2000; Banks, 1993a). The inclusion of a wider variety of texts without a concomitant shift in pedagogical practices is not sufficient, as illustrated in the following example.

In a fascinating study, Kaomea (2003) analyzed the *kupana* program in the public schools of Hawai'i, a program established in 1980 in response to a state mandate to teach indigenous culture, history, and language. Her research illustrates the limitations of curricular reforms without pedagogical interventions. The *kupana* program was developed in response to the ban on teaching the native Hawai'ian language 'Ōlelo Hawai'i in the public schools, a remnant of colonialization. The program sought to address this failure to teach the indigenous language and other aspects of native Hawai'ian cultures by bringing community elders, *kupunas*, into classrooms. The *kupunas* were instructed to teach a prescribed curriculum built around performances that included music, dance, singing, and crafts without addressing or teaching about the historical injustices related to language and rights. Kaomea found that the curriculum effectively erased the colonialist history under the guise of introducing the native "culture."

Although designed to remedy past injustices, the curriculum failed to address the political context, including the critical choices about content and the role of the indigenous language in teaching and learning. It was not enough simply to introduce indigenous practices; Kaomea (2003) argues that it was essential to address the racism implicit in the prior decision to ignore the linguistic and cultural resources of native Hawai'ians. This same critique can be applied to many attempts to bring multicultural perspectives and material into the curriculum. As illustrated in this chapter, it is not enough to shift the curriculum to reflect the heritages of the students. It is essential to infuse the multicultural curriculum with an analysis of power and tools for critique. Teaching students to use multi-modalities to compose texts is a first step in this process.

In the United States and throughout much of the world, teachers are required to implement mandated curricula that do not address these issues, including an analysis of power dynamics. As pointed out previously, many districts have frameworks that guide teachers with suggestions for content and sequencing; some include scripts for teachers to read and provide the expected student responses to teacher questions. Silence is not considered an acceptable response. Ms. Coleman taught in a school district with a recently mandated standardized curriculum, accompanied by external scripts and pacing guides that prescribed how and when material must be taught to students. A prominent feature of the district was its 6-week testing cycle, with 5 weeks of instruction, followed by 1 week of review and testing. The pressures to meet NCLB's Adequate Yearly Progress in this district and school have meant that the tests, including the yearly state assessments, have a strong influence on classroom practice. Every day and in each classroom, teaching and curriculum were aligned with skills that appeared on the benchmark and yearly tests.

When textbook editors and people in large central offices determine the curriculum, the content is removed from the immediate lives and interests of the students (Schultz & Fecho, 2005). Students' identities and lived experiences are frequently absent from such classrooms, which focus instead on covering mandated material and test preparation. The immense pressure from the tests makes it practically impossible for teachers to make any other pedagogical choices or to pay attention to the meanings of students' responses that might include silence, constraining opportunities for learning. The focus on a standardized curriculum leaves little room for classroom practice that reflects the lives of students in the classroom, incorporation of the immediate local context, and recognition of a wider variety of ways to participate in school.

As I describe in this chapter, despite the limitations of a mandated curriculum, Ms. Coleman made a tremendous effort to construct a curriculum that reflected the lives, experiences, and cultural understandings of the children in her classroom. She consistently drew connections for the students between their lives, her own experiences, current events in the world, including popular culture, and the school texts. In other words, one way that she attempted to address the potential silences of students in response to the narrow curriculum was by soliciting students' stories and perspectives. Despite—or perhaps because of—this practice, there were still students whose contributions were frequently missing from the classroom discourse community.

Throughout this book, I urge educators to count silence as participation when it reflects engagement, while at the same time noticing how that silence is interactionally achieved. If students are actively engaged in a classroom activity and choose to remain silent, I urge teachers to understand that silence as a form of participation. Importantly, working with the students themselves, I urge teachers to investigate a student's decision to remain silent, a topic I explore in greater depth in the next chapter. There are times when teachers are able to recognize student silence as a form of engagement, marking the student as a participatory student, whose silence is a sign of participation. At other times, such as when teachers focus on talk as an indication of learning, silence does not mark an engaged student and instead signals disinterest, resistance, or some other stance. The curriculum of multimodal storytelling provides opportunities for alternative modes of participation for students, giving them ways to engage in the classroom through modalities other than talk or silence. In particular, this chapter investigates questions such as:

- What are ways for teachers to address students' silence through pedagogical practices and curriculum change?
- What are possible responses for teachers when students take on a stance of silence?
- What are other avenues for their participation?
- Finally, how does the introduction of multimodalities allow students to attain a participatory presence in the classroom?

After introducing the research project that brought my colleagues and me into the classroom, I begin with a more elaborate description of how Ms. Coleman connected the curriculum in her classroom to students' lives. I use the analysis of pedagogical practices, curricular decisions, and multimodal texts to illustrate the arguments of the chapter that suggest the importance of providing students with multiple avenues of expression and participation.

CLASSROOM CONTEXT AND CURRICULUM INTERVENTION

As part of a longitudinal research project, I worked closely with Amelia Coleman and several graduate students for 4 years to develop a process we came to call multimodal storytelling. From the beginning, we worked closely with Ms. Coleman, a former graduate student at my university, to articulate the research questions and goals of the project and to design the classroom activities, and data collection and analysis. In this project, researchers often acted as teachers, working closely with the students in a range of ways throughout the school year. Likewise, as the classroom teacher, Ms. Coleman was intimately involved in formulating research questions, data collection, and the ongoing analysis that characterized our iterative research process.

The research team strategically introduced four interconnected projects that formed the centerpiece of the research. These projects were designed to complement the teacher's curricular plan for her students and the district curriculum, and to provide multiple avenues for student expression that went beyond typical written texts and standardized assessments. We aligned the projects with the mandated curriculum so that Ms. Coleman could use each of the projects to reinforce the strategies the children were responsible for on the benchmark tests administered every 6 weeks, while at the same time drawing on more accessible texts and forms of expression. For instance, a strategy from the district reading curriculum was "finding details." In one project, students were instructed to tell stories from photographs, which we then used to ask them to identify details for their writing. As another example, we asked the students to tell stories reflected in photographs from a variety of perspectives to reinforce the reading strategy of identifying points of view. We consciously designed activities that highlighted textual, visual, and aural modes of composition, including a final integrative project to create a movie with iMovie software. Ms. Coleman designated time for these multimodal projects to be integrated into the curriculum throughout each school year and, over the 4 years, gradually took the lead in some of the projects.

The introductory activity, which used written texts as the primary modality, was the creation of "Where I'm From" poems, adapted from a writing lesson described by Linda Christensen (2000). We originally included this activity to give the students opportunities and tools to draw on their home lives to write texts, especially poetry. In addition, we wanted the students to think critically about representation and, in particular, how aspects of their lives—such as familiar foods or sayings—could be connected to school learning.

The second modality focused on visual representations. For this project, called "Buildings Speak," students went on neighborhood walks with the goal of identifying buildings that held stories. After students selected and photographed the buildings, they captured stories on digital recorders that they later transcribed, expanded, and revised several times using the photographs and oral renditions of the stories. Students took pictures of a variety of contexts, including their own apartments, their favorite stores and neighborhood gathering places, and their school. For instance, one student photographed a store called "Sassy Beauty," a discount store for girls.

She told a story of running into the store to escape boys and then shopping there with her sister, defining the store as a distinctly female space. The buildings held personal, family, school, and community stories and memories, both profound and mundane, often leading to powerful, humorous, and touching pieces of writing.

The third project, "Soundscapes," was designed to give students opportunities to tell stories through various types of sounds. One year, Ms. Coleman chose historical themes connected to her curriculum and students brought in music and searched on the Web for sounds that told stories and represented ideas related to these themes. For instance, students compiled music and sounds to compose stories about authors such as Langston Hughes and Patricia Polacco, the activist Rosa Parks, and the athlete Roberto Clemente. Another year, they gathered neighborhood sounds to tell stories of their lives and experiences through sound. For example, they collected sounds from a neighborhood grocery store that prompted a story about shopping with parents at the end of a long, busy day (Schultz, Vasudevan, Bateman, & Coleman, 2004).

As a culminating project for this yearlong curriculum, students drew on a variety of modes—visual and aural—in order to compose a story about themselves as readers and writers using the iMovie video editing software. To make these movies, students collected photographs from their homes and community, music, and texts, including writing from the school year. Some years, Ms. Coleman used the movies as a type of portfolio or collection of artifacts for students to reflect back on their year and set goals or aspirations for their future. More concretely, students often looked through their writing from the year to uncover themes and actual pieces of writing to use in the movies. We provided students with simple equipment to collect materials. For instance, we gave them disposable cameras to take pictures to add to the stories (since digital technology, including cell phones with cameras, was not yet widely available). One student took pictures of all the places in her home where she liked to read and write. Another took pictures of basketball courts. A third focused on his grandmother, describing her role in his life and her influence on him. In addition, the students collected a range of music, including compact discs and music available on the Internet. Finally, they wrote new texts and selected writing from across the year. Beginning with a written text or set of essays, or alternatively with pictures or music, students used the movie software to compose a layered multimodal story that incorporated written text, pictures, and sounds.

We called the sequence of activities multimodal storytelling to distinguish it from digital storytelling, which is a specific process with a more prescribed sequence of steps, usually beginning with a written script

(Vasudevan, Schultz, & Bateman, under review; see also Hull & James, 2007). We wanted students to select initial or lead modalities to use in order to tell their stories. For instance, while many students chose to begin by writing their stories, later adding pictures and words, other students began with a set of photographs or, more rarely, with music. Their multimodal stories were often deeply personal stories about their lives and ambitions. This decision to write personal stories may have been made in response to the prompts the students were given by the researchers and Ms. Coleman. Alternatively, the students may have told these personal stories because of the project's emphasis on collecting a wide range of artifacts from their lives outside of school. Although the researchers often worked with small groups of the students to assist the classroom teacher, we attempted to weave the projects into the fabric of the class curriculum. We purposefully kept the equipment simple—using disposable cameras, for instance—in order to make it feasible for the classroom teacher to integrate the projects into her classroom once she did not have the added resources from the research project. We did not set out to understand this as a curricular intervention for students who were silent or invisible in the classroom. Instead, over time, we came to understand that some students who rarely participated in the verbal exchanges of typical classroom activities found ways to express themselves through the multiple modalities we introduced in this project.

CONNECTING CURRICULUM TO STUDENTS' LIVES

Early in one school year, Ms. Coleman introduced "Where I'm From" poems, an activity she had learned through her work with the research team. She initiated the poetry writing lesson by dividing a piece of chart paper into four squares and labeling those squares *food*, *sayings*, *memories*, and *people* in order to collect ideas for the poem. Sharing her own life experiences as examples of each of these categories, she modeled the activity. After Ms. Coleman explained that she was from a family who eats collard greens and candied yams, she added that she is also from a time when she ate cereal without milk. She used this example to encourage the students to write about authentic, and even intimate, events, as illustrated in the following dialogue.

> Ms. Coleman: I'm from cereal with no milk because I am from hard times. Is it okay to talk about being from hard times?
> Students: Yes.
> Ms. Coleman: Do you think I'm okay right now?

STUDENTS: Yes.

MS. COLEMAN: Sometimes it's good to acknowledge being from hard times because it makes you stronger. Are any of you from hard times?

STUDENTS: (nods and silence)

MS. COLEMAN (after a brief pause): It's not your fault you have to be from hard times because that's the way life is sometimes. (field notes & videotape, 9/12/05)

Ms. Coleman found many opportunities like this one to draw connections between her own experiences growing up in a comparable neighborhood to that of her students and to their experiences as African American youth growing up in low-income households. She believed it was important to integrate their knowledge and interests with the mandated district curriculum. She frequently used her own life experiences, accomplishments, and beliefs as illustrative examples, acting as a role model for the majority of students who were African American and shared her racial and class background. The increasing standardization of curriculum across the country geared to high-stakes testing makes it less likely that teachers have the time or opportunities to forge these connections. Although she taught in a district with a locally mandated curriculum, Ms. Coleman, like many talented teachers, found many moments to adapt the curriculum to her students. At the same time, these projects were severely limited by the pressure exerted by the high-stakes testing that narrowed the kinds of participation structures and the types of knowledge and evidence of learning in the classroom.

Although at first glance the racial composition of the class reflected that of most schools in this urban district whose student bodies are 98% African American, a closer look at its racial and ethnic composition revealed greater diversity, including several students who were recent immigrants from Nigeria, Sierra Leone, Jamaica, the Dominican Republic, Cambodia, and Bangladesh, among several other countries. Throughout the school, more than 20 languages were spoken. African and Caribbean immigrant students made up a significant percentage of the English Language Learners (ELL) population in the school. While many immigrant students who emigrated from West Africa spoke variations of French, Caribbean students—mostly from Jamaica, where the official language is English—were also placed in ELL classes because of their distinct Creole and accent. In the final years of the study, the number of students from West Africa and the Caribbean increased (Schultz & Coleman, 2009).

Ms. Coleman structured her classroom teaching around the mandated curriculum, while at the same time, she found ways to introduce literature and ideas that drew on the localized knowledge that students—and, in particular, the African American students—brought to the classroom. She believed in "a flexible curriculum where teachers have a chance to really think about what would work for [a] particular group of kids, but still having standards and having things be aligned with standards" (interview, 12/06/05). Given the diversity of heritages, cultures, and languages that students brought to the classroom, it was often difficult for Ms. Coleman to find common ground for the classroom conversations. Although she provided many opportunities for students to tell stories about their lives, there were students who did not connect as readily with the central class assignments or with the stories and life lessons that Ms. Coleman incorporated into her practice. There were many ways that Ms. Coleman understood the textures and struggles that were part of the experiences of every student in her classroom. At the same time, the intimate connections she was able to forge with the African American students may have been more remote for the immigrant students. At the beginning of the study, immigrant students comprised about 10% of the class; by the end, they accounted for close to 20% of the students.

Building on the work of Dewey and other progressive educators in the United States, over the past century, teachers have found ways to develop curriculum by attending to students' interests and lived realities (Levy, 1996; Skilton-Sylvester, 1994). As I argue elsewhere (Schultz, 2003), it is essential—although not always enough—for classrooms to reflect students' lives with books and materials that reflect their interests and heritage. In addition, I suggest that teachers learn how to listen and respond with deep understanding to their students, as Ms. Coleman did, and endeavor to bring their students' lives into the classroom. However, it may not have been enough for Ms. Coleman to ask the students to tell stories about their lives and write poems that reflect their heritages in order for them to participate in school learning, as illustrated in the following vignette.

> On the third day of school, rather than using the mandated text, Ms. Coleman read the picture book *Skin Again* (hooks, 2004) to the class in order to teach the designated skill of prediction. She opened the lesson by asking the students to predict the themes of the book by looking at the cover: a drawing of black and white hands clasped together. As she read the book aloud, she paused to emphasize the sentence "The skin I'm in is just a covering . . . it can't tell my story, if you want to know who I am you've got to come inside" (p. 10). After a lively discussion about the book, Ms. Coleman asked the class, "How do you think we will practice doing

this in here, looking inside of one another?" Without waiting for a response, she continued, "I want a chance to know who you are. I want to look into you. I want to get a chance to look into our histories." (field notes & videotape, 9/8/05)

Ms. Coleman's careful choice of texts and activities invited students to bring their knowledge into the curriculum, pointing to issues that were salient in their lives. She listened closely to their stories, acknowledging the particularities of each child and what each brought to the classroom (Schultz, 2003). Supplementing the materials created by publishers without localized knowledge of students' lives, she drew on her own experiences and connections to the students to engage them in learning. Despite this effort, in some years, the recent immigrant students were noticeably quiet during these kinds of activities. The discussion of race and skin color prompted by the children's book *Skin Again* and the lesson on predictions seemed to engender silence from this group of students.

"Race" may be understood and discussed differently by different groups of students from across a range of backgrounds. Most of the recent immigrant students in the classroom were from places where the majority of the population is Black, making it likely that this mode of conversation about race and skin color was unfamiliar to them. An assumption of critical multicultural education is that explicit discussions of topics such as "race" are key components of more inclusive classrooms. Ms. Coleman combined a focus on a reading strategy with an effort to build the classroom community through the discussion of an issue that is central to the lives of many people of color. Her goal was to provide students with an opportunity to use their own knowledge and experience to engage in academic tasks, drawing on her shared background with a majority of the students in the classroom. However, despite the similarity in their racial backgrounds, it may have been difficult for the small number of students without the same experience of racial diversity in U.S. contexts or with different understandings of "race" to respond to the text and make accurate predictions. Their silence during the lesson reflected a possible disjuncture between their experiences and those of the majority of the students in the class.

It would have been difficult for Ms. Coleman to find literature and stories from the countries of origin and ethnicities of all of the students in her classroom, especially given the limitations placed on her teaching by the standardized curriculum. Instead, she relied on the students themselves to bring their stories into the classrooms and gave them a few ways to do this. The "Where I'm From" poem that was a part of the multimedia storytelling project is one such example. Ms. Coleman also worked to weave examples from popular culture into her lessons. For instance, one day, she used the artist Fifty Cent as an example in a lesson on plurals, pointing out his decision not to put an "s" at the end of his name. These curriculum choices did not address student silence in the classroom. In order to reach all students in the class, she learned that she needed to go beyond these examples and the activities that encouraged the students to tell their stories. When some students were reluctant to contribute stories, she shifted participation structures and found other ways to open up the curriculum to more students, including those who were typically silent.

ADDRESSING STUDENT SILENCE THROUGH MULTIMODALITIES

The class was working on another lesson to reinforce the strategy of making predictions. After reading a short portion of a story from the district-mandated textbook, Ms. Coleman asked the class to tell her how their predictions about the story changed as they read the text. She called on Sherry, who characteristically shrugged and said, "I don't know." Ms. Coleman informed Sherry that she would return to her to learn her predictions, asking the rest of the class whether or not they remembered their initial predictions. Later, when Sherry continued to protest about sharing her prediction aloud, Ms. Coleman reminded her, "Don't forget when we come to school we come to learn, and part of learning is being prepared to share . . . if we don't talk, if we don't ask questions, if we don't share what's in our brains, are we able to fully learn?" The class answered her rhetorical question in unison, saying, "No!" Ms. Coleman continued, "That's why I give you the chance to think about what you're going to share before I ask you to share. Didn't I ask you to write them down? I didn't put you on the spot, did I?" Again, the students responded as a chorus, "No." Ms. Coleman turned to the students who were willing to share their predictions and continued the lesson. (field notes, 9/6/05)

Ms. Coleman often varied the participation structures of her classroom to make the curriculum more accessible to the students. For instance, she allowed students to choose a classmate to read their story aloud if they were too shy to read in front of the group. She also gave them opportunities to work in pairs and occasionally small groups, as described above, often asking them to write down their thoughts before she asked them to speak aloud. Sometimes this was not enough, as Sherry's silence illustrates. The reasons for Sherry's silence were complex and may have included the need for more time and space or a desire to protect herself from the scrutiny of others.

Although Ms. Coleman reinforced the idea that students were expected to share their thoughts as members of the classroom community, the immigrant students were noticeably absent from verbal participation in lessons. As explained in Chapter 2, their silence often reflected their difficulty in expressing thoughts through a new language, their need for more time, and, perhaps, their desire to protect their home lives from the gaze of their classmates and teacher. Although Ms. Coleman generally offered students two modes of participation—oral and written—the introduction of multimodal storytelling offered students multiple entry points for contributing to the classroom conversation and the curriculum and for enacting new ways of being a student.

Ben: Becoming More Visible in the Classroom

Seated at his desk in his fifth-grade classroom on a warm September day, Ben conjured up memories of Cambodia. It was not difficult for him to begin his "Where I'm From" poem. He was reminded every day of where he is from; that aspect of his identity was central to how he introduced himself to his teacher and peers in his urban public school. He began with his own title, "I Am From," and continued mixing and blending his old and new worlds:

> I am from killing fields, animals all around, riding bikes, and
>   shared love.
> I am from rice, egg rolls, and noodles. I am from DVDs and
>   songs and cd's, movies and model cars.
> I am from poor and rich. I am from sickness and hardness.
> I am from a loving heart and grandparents love of us part.
> I am from the flag that I love. The flag is of the love in our
>   country. I am from red and blue. I am from Cambodia.

Later in the year, Ben was given a different, yet related assignment to compose a multimodal story. Through images, words, and music, Ben and his classmates represented where they were from, what they experienced during their fifth-grade year in school, and their aspirations for the future in this cumulative project. Once again, Ben turned to his family and his home country as a source of ideas. He brought into school a single drawing from home of his grandfather, who died recently in Cambodia, images and maps from a computer, and several photographs. The drawing exemplified his respect for this relative and represented the essence of who he is and where he is from. The map of Cambodia located his story in a geographical place. The photographs contextualized his life. He selected Cambodian music and narrated a story into an audio recorder. His final project, a 2-minute narrative composed with iMovie software on a computer, captured his past, present, and future in a dream-like sequence that embodied the sadness he had carried with him throughout the year (Schultz, 2006b).

Teachers often encounter students who do not have words to express their experiences or, for a variety of reasons, choose not to speak these words aloud, as described in Chapter 2. They may be so distanced from these experiences that they do not have access to words to describe them. As a result, teachers are greeted with silence, blank papers, and shrugs. Ben was often silent in the classroom. The chance to write a poem about his experiences and later to integrate the experiences and images into a digital narrative or a multimodal story using iMovie software gave him new opportunities for participation in the academic life of the classroom. The introduction of multimodalities gave Ben the opportunity to express his ideas and knowledge outside of conventional textual practices, which may have been more difficult for him as a recent English Language Learner. He used his "Where I'm From" poem to integrate his current life in Philadelphia with his family heritage. The focus on telling stories through images and music allowed Ben and his classmates to tell stories that varied from those traditionally written or told in school (Schultz & Coleman, 2009; Vasudevan, 2004; Vasudevan, Schultz, & Bateman, under review).

Outside of school, many youth, especially those in urban areas, have opportunities to experiment and compose with multiple modalities, performing spoken-word poetry, displaying narratives in digital videos, and composing graphic novels, zines, fan fiction, and elaborate video games (cf., Gee, 2003; Thomas, 2004). These media are powerful pedagogical tools, filled with learning, exploration, and possibilities for many youth. In contrast, all too frequently, students only read and compose paper-based printed texts inside school. Students are rarely invited to bring their out-of-school knowledge, writing, and interests into the classroom because these aspects of their lives do not easily fit into the mandated daily lessons or the routinized modes of school participation. Adding multimodalities to the curriculum provides students with more opportunities to become engaged in school, opening up new possibilities for their participation.

In our interviews and discussions, there were various reasons that the immigrant students and other quieter students gave for why they did not verbally participate in the classroom. Some were simply shy. Others worried about their lack of facility with English or their discomfort with the pace of the classroom conversations. Still other students were preoccupied or disengaged from the content of classroom talk. Some students did not want to talk in front of their peers because they did not want to appear to be too engaged in school. Multimodal storytelling introduced a curriculum that focused on new ways to compose stories, placing students' lives at the center. It may have been easier for a student like Ben to bring in a picture that represented his grandfather in Cambodia than to compose and read a story aloud, especially one about such a personal topic. Cambodian music may have conveyed emotions that he did not have words to describe. Hull (2003) argues for the salience of multimodalities, suggesting, "Ours is an age in which the pictoral turn has supplanted the linguistic one, as images push words off the page and our lives becomes increasingly mediated by a popular visual culture" (p. 230). Visual images dominate the landscape; music permeates many people's lives. These modes can be significant resources for students as they compose stories in school. Rather than replacing silence, multimodal storytelling gave students a way to translate their silence into stories. For students who were often silent, the multimodal stories gave them a way to mark themselves as engaged and participatory students.

Saima: Claiming a Participatory Presence

In this classroom, where the teacher valued the importance of making connections to students' lives and communities, opportunities to compose stories through multimodal storytelling enabled a group of students to become more visible through sharing their knowledge and details of their lives in different modalities without placing themselves front and center in the classroom. In composing these stories and reading or projecting them on a screen for their teacher and peers, some students were able to step outside of their roles as "silent," "quiet," or "disengaged" to embrace a wider set of ways to be a student in school. In particular, the students who were recent immigrants and quieter than their classmates for a variety of reasons used the multimedia projects to have a stronger, more visible, and participatory presence in the classroom and take on different roles as students. This is illustrated by Saima's engagement and growth through the multimodal projects.

Saima was a studious, quiet, and small Bengali girl who wore a *parda* (headscarf) and described herself as "timid." She had arrived in the United States during her fourth-grade year and had only been in the country for several months when she entered this classroom. From the beginning, it was clear that Saima strove to perform well in her academic work, and, as

Ms. Coleman observed, she showed tremendous improvement in her reading and writing as she rapidly learned a new language and a new way to
be a student.

For the initial assignment of the multimodal storytelling project, Saima
wrote these five sentences to describe her background as the opening to
her "Where I'm From" poem:

> I am from chicken, fish, and rice. From fighting, jogging, and
> running. I am from French fries, fried chicken, and chicken nug-
> gets. From talking, laughing, and joking. I am from trees, bushes,
> and flowers.

In this initial poem, Saima wrote about her life in somewhat generic terms,
describing herself as being "from chicken, fish, and rice." Her writing contained the requisite elements for this poetic genre; however, it lacked speci-
ficity and did not seem reflective of the particularities of Saima's life,
perhaps because she was in the process of acquiring fluency in English. In
its generalities and precision, it mirrored much of her writing up until that
date in the classroom. Her description of eating "French fries, fried chicken,
and chicken nuggets" reflected her Americanized life since immigrating
to the United States, her still halting use of English, and her attempts to
conform to the norms set by her classmates. This poem, written early in
the school year, suggests the constraints that Saima may have felt in composing a written text for a school assignment. She was compliant in following the instructions, yet she may have decided to hide aspects of her
home and family life in order to blend into the unstated norms of the classroom. Many students made this same choice to protect their home life or
draw a boundary between home and school for a variety of understandable and important reasons. Given the parameters of the assignment,
however, we were surprised by Saima's decision not to include aspects of
her Bengali heritage in the poem. There were sections of the writing that
seemed disconnected from our knowledge of Saima's background, as reflected in another section of the same poem:

> I am from country music, and country movies. From tag, hide and
> seek, and freeze tag. I am from car, bus, and trucks. From winter,
> summer, and fall.

Rather than using this project to explore her heritage, as Ben and many
of her classmates did, Saima seemed to opt to complete the assignment by
simply following directions. Although it is plausible that her family listened
to country music, the three seasons she wrote about did not seem to re-

flect her life growing up in South Asia. This assignment was designed to draw on students' knowledge and experiences, and did not seem to capture Saima's imagination; she treated it like other, more scripted, assignments during the year.

In contrast, a few months later, Saima used her "Buildings speak" writing—a project that added a visual component to a more conventional writing assignment—to tell a personal story about her arrival in this country as a new immigrant. Instead of a formulaic story, she told a story that held meaning for her, which may have shifted her engagement in school projects. Paired with an image of her best friend's bedroom window, Saima's soft voice narrated a story of how she initially approached this friend after hearing her speak Bengali:

> Hi, my name is [Saima]. I took a picture of my friend's house because first when I came to America, I didn't know nobody and I didn't know how to speak English. Then I saw them, I thought they were my country's people and I talked to them and finally became best friends. And that's why I took the picture.

The simplicity of the words and photograph convey an important moment that connected Saima's home and school experiences in a story

Figure 4.1. Saima's Buildings Speak project

that transcended the words and images. Throughout the subsequent projects that involved composing with a variety of digital modalities, Saima's transnational narrative continued to evolve. For her culminating project, Saima composed a multimedia story in which she brought together several threads of a single story through digital artifacts that represented various aspects of her identity. As we watched and listened to this story, we were struck by the ways that Saima's acquisition of a louder voice in the classroom coincided with the availability of a wider range of modalities with which to participate.

As the students explored various digital modalities to represent themselves, Saima began to include new and different details in her texts. Ms. Coleman gave the students three questions for their end-of-the-year portfolio to prompt the students to reflect on what they brought to the classroom from their homes and communities, what they had learned during their fifth-grade year, and their future goals. She wanted the students to document what they had learned along with their goals, to motivate them to continue to work hard in school after they left her classroom. To begin her movie project, Saima composed three texts in response to these three questions: Where Am I From, Who Am I, and Where Am I Going?

These new pieces of writing were markedly different from her initial "Where I'm From" poem, enriched by her simultaneous use of visual images, music, and her own voice narrating the text. The section composed in response to the question "Where Am I From" opened with the following line: "No one can take away from me, my name, for it is mine. Bengali am I." The poem continued:

> I am the river that flows
> Through my land.
> I am the mountain
> Royal and wonderful
> Rising up out of the confusion and end
> I greet the morning sun
> That shines down on my rich valleys
> And dries my empty waste.
> I am the red poppy and yellow saying
> That grow upon my bleeding hills.
> I am the battle cry of freedom
> That repeats through my hallways
> And every grain of my being.
> Therefore, I am.
> No one can take my name

Away from me,
Not tanks or guns or bombs
Meant to abuse me and kill me.
My country lives in me.
I am the cry of liberty
No matter what they take from me,
They can't take away my name
Or my dignity.
Bengali am I

In the poem and throughout the movie, Saima claimed her national identity as she recounted her past and present and imagined her future. Her
words and images are significant departures from her descriptions of eating chicken nuggets and listening to country music in her initial poem at
the beginning of the year. In her multimodal story, Saima's soft, yet strong
voice narrated a layered story of her family that connected to her imagined future as a doctor. The poetry, writing, photographs, and movie all
gave Saima the tools to tell her story. When she entered into the storytelling
process through the modes of image and sound, Saima's texts became more
complex and powerful. She translated her quiet compliance into a louder,
more participatory presence.

By extending the composing process beyond print modalities, students' compositions changed in significant ways. Beginning with various modalities such as digital photography and music generated different
ways to tell stories and led to the construction of new and layered texts
(Vasudevan, Schultz, & Bateman, under review). Offering a range of
digital composing modalities to students allowed them to document and
include elements of themselves that either could not be or were not reflected in their written texts or their verbal participation in class. At the
beginning of the year, Saima's voice was barely audible when she spoke.
In place of reading a story out loud, her multimodal story was projected
on the wall with her voice transmitted through the speakers connected
to the computer. The new modalities gave her new ways to mark herself as a participatory student in the class without the need to speak loudly
while standing alone in the front of the room. When she entered the storytelling process through images and music, Saima's authorial voice grew
in volume and depth. Previously, she had written in solitude without
the benefit of her classmates' input. Through these new opportunities,
Saima became engaged in classroom activities as an exemplary participant. Had the modes of participation been limited to talk, it seems less
likely that she would have taken on this role.

Michael: Claiming an Academic Presence

It was not only immigrant students who benefited from the introduction of multimodal storytelling in this classroom. Michael was an outgoing and energetic African American boy who was only periodically engaged in school assignments. His investment and attentiveness in the classroom was highly dependent on the amount of personal attention he received from teachers and other adults in the classroom. There were long periods of silence when Michael was disengaged from the daily work of the classroom. His silence represented a kind of resistance to schoolwork that seemed unattainable to him because of its difficulty and its distance from topics he cared about. However, in contrast to his sparse writing for classroom assignments, Michael wrote a powerful story to accompany the picture of his apartment building for the "Buildings Speak" project. This was one of the first assignments that seemed to capture his attention.

For this project, Michael chose to photograph the entryway and front steps leading to his apartment. This photograph held stories that reflected his activities inside and outside his home. After taking a few pictures, Michael sat on the steps and recorded his conflicting feelings about life in his neighborhood.

> I lived in my building for 8 years now. When I first moved around here, everybody that I saw was all bigger than me and I was only 2. And I started going outside with my big brother and anybody that messed with me, he would take care of me. He would stick up for me. And so, as I got older, everybody just started playing with me and stuff. But sometimes it makes me want to move because every night while people trying to have fun, you hear gunshots and everything. And when you come outside in the morning on the way to school, you see traces around people dead body, traces around bullets and stuff. And sometimes it make me want to stay 'cause all my friends is here. And we always play football and basketball out back . . . that's my story.

In his story, Michael noted that he had grown from a small child who was new to the building to a boy with many friends who shared his desire to play sports all day long on the sidewalk. Simultaneously, he pointed out the persistent violence in his community that made him wish he could move away. Michael had never before expressed this kind of commitment and thoughtfulness in his school writing.

Figure 4.2. Michael's Buildings Speak project

Through a photograph and recorded narrative, Michael composed a powerful story rooted in a particular geography and reflective of his deep connection to family and friends (Hull & James, 2007). He characterized his neighborhood using disparate terms, conveying both his experiences of happiness and his desire, at times, to leave his community. Central to the narrative is the idea of relationship and protection reflected in his initial reference to his brother and his mention of his friends in the final sentence. It is notable that he concluded with an upbeat statement, a stance that characterized much of his composing that year. An honest description of the world that he experienced replaced his characteristic silence and disaffection for academics. It was not that he was a quiet student. Michael was quite the opposite—boisterous and often distracting to his classmates. In contrast, when asked to complete academic tasks prior to this experience, Michael was generally withdrawn and wrote very little. His stance toward academics and his reluctance to invest himself in school learning reflected a particular kind of silence that kept him from becoming engaged in his schoolwork. The loud, disruptive behavior acted as a cover for his academic silence.

Through curricular opportunities to compose multimodal stories, students like Michael—whose school performance did not reflect the richness of their literate traditions at home or their abilities as storytellers—are better positioned to be welcomed into learning rather than pushed out to the margins. The availability of multiple modalities and the opportunity to draw on his community and home life meant that Michael traded blank pages and a disengaged attitude in class for periods of time where he produced work that displayed his knowledge, perspectives on the world, and considerable talents.

For Michael, as for many of his classmates, his school writing represented only a fraction of his texts and did not often draw on the richness of his home- and community-based identities and communicative resources (Schultz, 2003). Multimodal storytelling allowed Michael to connect these contexts and take risks in his composing. Throughout the rest of the school year, Michael drew on his "Buildings Speak" project and developed a narrative that conveyed the importance of his family to his identity as a learner and composer of stories. Themes such as family, sports, friends, and the neighborhood all reappeared in his final multimodal story, signified by photographs, narration, and music (Vasudevan, Schultz, & Bateman, under review). The projects connected to the multimodal storytelling allowed Michael to claim an academic presence in school—one more closely aligned with engagement in academic tasks, replacing disaffected silence with participation.

Michael was generally loud, although his talk was often not focused on academic assignments. Like many of his classmates, his mind was more often on basketball, events in his neighborhood, or the playground than the official content of the classroom. The opportunity to draw on his home experiences shifted Michael's participation in his classroom. Rather than giving him a louder voice or participatory presence, as was true for Saima and Ben, it enabled him to become more engaged in the academic or official classroom activities. Opening up the curriculum to multimodal storytelling made the curriculum more accessible to students like Michael and changed the nature of their participation in official classroom events.

CONCLUSION: OPENING UP THE CURRICULUM TO ALL STUDENTS

Who has the right to speech? Who has the right to silence? (Stein, 2004)

Exploring many of the themes in this chapter, Stein (2004), a South African educator, writes about multimodal pedagogies, which she explains are critical to education in this post-apartheid country. She explains that in South Africa, as in much of the world, the dominant modes of communication are oral; radio and television are more common than written texts or print media. This preference for non-text-based forms of communication places particular kinds of demands on teachers who must mediate between the focus on written literacy in schools and common modes of communication outside of school. The depth of tragedy and unspeakable events in South Africa's past present specific and contextual challenges to teachers and leaders.

Stein (2004) explains the role of silence as a form of communication, pointing out the possibilities engendered by the introduction of multimodalities that are similar to those I describe in Ms. Coleman's classroom:

> In multimodal pedagogies, silence as a mode of communication has the materiality of sound without volume; it has rhythm and variation. It is a mode that is participatory, affirmative, and productive rather than oppositional and resistant. Using silence in pedagogy is not to disadvantage any group. This is an inclusive silence, rather than excluding or threatening, allowing for a positivity and presence of being. This silence acknowledges learners as subjects of integrity who may want teachers to "hear" that there are things that are unspeakable, which cannot be said. (p. 113)

In Chapter 2, I described the silence enacted by students in response to unspeakable events in their lives. For instance, Ma-Lee, a Hmong student, held onto silence until her teacher created a space for informal talk that had different norms for participation (Campano, 2007). Drawing on this same understanding of the role of silence, Stein suggests that the opportunity to choose silence allows students to decide whether or not to speak, giving them authority over their texts. The availability of silence as a form of participation allows students to select which stories they tell out loud and which stories or horrors they keep to themselves. She emphasizes further that the possibility of responding through silence is positive and inclusive rather than a barrier that protects and excludes others. Elaborating the concept that some ideas are ineffable and expressed in ways other than through words, Stein (2004) writes, "Bodies hold history, memory, thought, feeling, and desires. Bodies hold language and silence. Our bodies are repositories of knowledge, but these knowledges are not always knowable in and through language—they can be felt, imagined, imaged or dreamed" (p. 99). It may be that it is necessary for ideas to remain private and encased in silence. Alternatively, multimodal pedagogies or ways of teaching that include the use of multimodal texts enable students to find forms to express these ideas, allowing them to join the classroom community.

As with the students in Stein's classroom, the introduction of multimodal storytelling created new opportunities and spaces for students in Ms. Coleman's classroom to attain a presence and to choose whether and how to contribute their stories to the larger community. Multimodal story-telling allowed Ben, Saima, Michael, and several of their classmates to recognize the value of their stories as they discovered and used new tools to convey them to a public audience. Rather than being disadvantaged by their silence or inability to put their ideas and feelings into written text read aloud to the group, they were provided with new ways to tell their stories without the pressure of speaking in front of a group. They were given opportunities to draw on knowledge that mattered to them to compose new kinds of stories. They each experienced events in their lives that were laced with complicated feelings that were difficult to express in words alone. In other contexts, they may have been disadvantaged by their lack of facility with language or academic knowledge. They may have used silence to garner extra time to reflect on questions. However, through multimodal storytelling, the additional modalities provided new avenues for participation in modes that extended to the whole class, reaching many of the original goals of multicultural education.

In Ms. Coleman's classroom, the curriculum project of multimodal storytelling brought new voices into the classroom. Students could stand silently while their stories were played aloud on the audio recorder or projected on a screen. Their stories could enter into classroom discourse without their standing in front of the group, which is difficult for some students—especially when the story is personal, when they are unsure of their language skills or accent, when they are shy, or for a variety of other reasons.

If one of the purposes of schooling is to open up opportunities and present students with broad access to knowledge and tools to pursue their goals, then it is important to find ways to engage as many students as possible in learning, providing a variety of ways for them to enter class-room activities. If classrooms are conceptualized as sites for young people to actively participate as citizens in a pluralistic democracy, then it is critical to expand the openings for students' participation. It is not enough simply to hear every person's voice in a classroom. It may not be suffi-cient, respectful, or desirable to solicit personal stories from every student with the assumption that intimacy and connectedness will come from the telling of these stories. Students, particularly those whose backgrounds may vary from the majority of students in the classroom and those who are initially shy or resistant to school, may need new invitations and modes in order to contribute to the classroom discourse. The arts offer alterna-tive modalities for student engagement in learning.

Maxine Greene (2003) reminds educators that the inclusion of the arts in education will nurture imaginations and build students' capacities for participation in a democracy:

> Teaching is possibility in dark and constraining times. It is a matter of awakening and empowering today's young people to name, to reflect, to imagine, and to act with more and more concrete responsibility in an increasingly multifarious world. . . . The light may be uncertain and flickering; but teachers in their lives and works have the remarkable capacity to make it shine in all sorts of corners, and, perhaps, to move newcomers to join with others, and transform. (pp. 72–73)

Talk is the central mode of participation in most classrooms. Through talk, teachers apprehend what students know and what they need to learn, illuminating possibilities in students' lives. Teachers' insistence that students participate through verbal modes is a successful strategy for most, although not all, students. In Amelia Coleman's classroom, multimodal storytelling allowed students who had been on the periphery of the classroom community because of their relative silence and outsider status to be marked as participatory students. In addition, connecting school learning to knowledge acquired in homes and the community allowed some, although not all, students to produce work that was meaningful to them. Through providing new modes for representing ideas and allowing content connected to students' lives in the classroom, Ms. Coleman built on students' strengths and capacities.

When educators find ways to listen closely to students and incorporate their voices into the classroom (Schultz, 2003), they focus on creating opportunities for students to draw on their own cultural knowledge from their families and communities. Students can use this knowledge as a foundation for learning new information and strategies, connecting their learning to what they know and care about. The curricular practice of multimodal storytelling is just one way to open up classrooms to more student participation and to draw on students' background experiences. By bringing together a focus on content and pedagogical practice, multimodal storytelling allows teachers to engage in new ways of teaching and representing knowledge that shifts who participates in classroom life and what their participation looks like. By creating opportunities for new perspectives and voices to enter into the classroom community, in part through her work with the multimodal storytelling project, Ms. Coleman was able to move from a focus on the majority of students in the classroom who shared her background to a more inclusive stance. Furthermore, the students themselves were able to learn from one another and gain a broader understanding of critical concepts that were deeply connected to their learning.

Student silence may contain meanings that teachers and peers can learn to read and understand. Although there may be moments when it is critical for students to hold on to their silence to protect themselves and create necessary boundaries around their home and community lives, there are also times when students do not verbally or actively participate in school because there are limited modes available to them. These conditions may deny them opportunities to learn and may curtail the learning of the whole class. The introduction of curricular and pedagogical practices that connect students' home and community knowledge with school learning opens up new opportunities for student participation. When Ms. Coleman told Sherry that if she is not talking she is not learning, she emphasized the importance of active participation. In this chapter, I argue that there are other ways to participate actively in the classroom community. At times, these might include silence. They also include composing stories through new modes and media and engaging in projects that connect community issues and knowledge to classroom learning.

During an interview, a student in Ms. Coleman's class explained, "Like, in my iMovie, I dealt with a passionate attitude with writing, a writer's passionate attitude." Often, emotions, particularly passion, are missing from school. With the advent of standardized curriculum, tightly scripted lessons, and high-stakes tests, there is little room for teachers to nurture students' passions and interests. Adding multimodalities to the curriculum and finding ways to engage students with issues that concern them or connect to their home and community lives opens up new possibilities for expression and engagement and allows them to find ways to contribute beyond their silence. Writing with a "passionate" attitude by using a variety of modalities holds new possibilities for shifting classroom practice and inviting more students to become visible members of the classroom community.

CHAPTER 5

Learning from Student Silence

A SMALL GROUP of prospective teachers in an elementary literacy methods course were sitting in a circle engaged in a literature discussion about a children's book, *Amazing Grace* (Hoffman, 1991). The book is about a young African American girl who loves to act and wants to play Peter in the class play *Peter Pan*. Even though one child says that she cannot be Peter because she is not a boy and another says she cannot play that role because she is Black, ultimately the girl is rewarded for her talent with the part. Each of the five small groups of student teachers read and discussed a different picture book that addressed a topic related to social inequality in order to prompt a discussion about how to incorporate critical and potentially difficult topics into classroom conversations. While they were engaged in the conversation, I asked the student teachers to note who spoke and who refrained from speaking and the various roles they each played in the literature discussion. As the individual book discussions came to a conclusion, I drew the whole class together, asking them to begin by writing about their experience. (field notes, 10/21/04)

My goal as the instructor in this class was to teach the prospective teachers how to use literature groups in their classrooms through participation in one. After we discussed the patterns of talk and silence in each of the small-group discussions, we brainstormed ways they might structure similar groups in their current elementary school classrooms. Next, I turned to the content of the books and asked them how and whether or not they might talk about the topics addressed by the books in their future classrooms. The group who read *Amazing Grace* commented that their discussion had focused on gender issues rather than on racial ones as I had anticipated. I asked them why this might be the case, as I had thought that the book highlighted race. There was an elongated silence. Noting aloud that there was only one African American participant in the group, I suggested that sometimes those kinds of discussions are more difficult across race lines. To frame this comment and prompt conversation, I drew on my experience with and research on leading discussions about race and desegregation with single- and mixed-race groups of middle school students (Schultz, Buck, & Niesz, 2000, 2005) and noted that some topics might be off limits in a multiracial context. A few students responded with brief comments; most remained silent.

Later that evening, I received an email from Carrie, the only African American student in that group. She said that she felt that my generalization about the difficulty of talking across race lines did not apply to her experience. Explaining to me that her sister-in-law is White, she said that she had discussions about race and racial dynamics all of the time with her sister-in-law and that they ventured into a wide range of topics. Furthermore, Carrie did not feel as though the teacher education classroom or her own elementary classroom, for that matter, was the appropriate place for such conversations. I was caught short by the email. In our urban-focused teacher education program at the University of Pennsylvania, where everyone teaches in city public schools that have majority populations of students of color, conversations about race and racism occur with some regularity. We assume that prospective teachers, especially those who have grown up in affluent, predominantly White suburbs, need to learn how to address these topics, among others, or at least have practice in doing so to prepare them to enter the predominantly Black and Latino urban classrooms that are dominant in our city.

As I considered the class discussion, I realized that rather than focusing on the teachers' silence about race during the book discussion, when there was a silence in our whole-class discussion, I had, perhaps too quickly, offered my own framing of the situation, without waiting and listening closely to what the prospective teachers might say. As I reviewed the interaction, I noticed that before I made the assertion, I had asked the group and then the class, "Why do you think there wasn't a conversation about race in this group?" When they responded with silence, I offered my hypothesis about the difficulty of such conversations. Lacking the tools in the moment to probe their silence in response to my question or to push the conversation further, I offered my own analysis and proceeded with the class. Although at other times explanations of my own research about conversations about race may have been useful for teachers, in this instance, my conjecture about the difficulty of conversations across race lines did not move the conversation forward. On the other hand, the email from the student prompted a generative conversation between the two of us and, ultimately, with others in the class that continued throughout the rest of the semester. Without that email, the conversation about silences would have been simply dropped (or silenced).

In my role as an educator, I seek to understand the silences in my classes at the whole-group level and also in relation to individual students. That same year, Alison, another prospective teacher, rarely spoke aloud.

She almost never talked in whole-group discussions and she never read her writing aloud to the entire class. Occasionally, she would contribute to small-group discussions, which were a daily occurrence, and I could usually hear her whispered voice in the short conversations between pairs of students that were another regular routine. Still, her voice and contributions were noticeably infrequent. There is often at least one quiet student in my classes at the beginning of the semester, but the participation structures are so varied and change so often that most students find venues for and modes of participation.

For instance, one student teacher recently commented that he was surprised to find himself making so many verbal contributions in our teacher education classes. As a college student, he rarely spoke, worried that he did not know as much as his peers. The difference, he explained, is that our teacher education program is built around a relatively small cohort who come to know one another through a variety of activities, including the classes they take together. He ventured that he had begun to speak in class because he felt known, which provided him with a measure of safety to speak and test out his ideas.

Sometimes in my teacher education classes, the silence seems to represent disengagement and a lack of interest; other times, it seems to represent fear. Most times, however, the prospective teachers get caught up in the activities and their voices enter the classroom community without their making a conscious decision about whether or not to speak. In contrast, Alison was persistently silent. I had individual conversations with her and talked to the whole group about the importance of both talking and not talking (stepping in and out of conversations), pointing out that some people might need to limit the amount they spoke to give others space to participate and explaining how they might learn to regulate their own talk as a way to learn to monitor the talk and silence in their own classrooms.

When Alison remained resolutely silent during most classes, my solution was to ask her to occasionally write an email to me about her reflections on the conversations in class so that I could gauge her understanding and engagement with the material. This solution did not bring her into dialogue with her classmates. In addition, it did not help me to understand why she chose silence, although she may not have wanted to talk about that. Over time, however, perhaps as a consequence of her practice through writing the email messages, I began to notice that she was willing to offer her opinion more frequently to the large group. Rather than a punishment, the private email correspondence helped to build a stronger relationship between the teacher and the student, which, over time, was translated into broader participation. I did not ask Alison to explain why she began to participate more frequently. I can speculate, however, that she gained confidence through these one-on-one interactions, that we developed trust with one another, and that the email exchanges provided her with practice and a space to try out her ideas, allowing her to verbally enter into the public space of the classroom.

Teachers of school-age youth and university students are often confronted by silent classes and silent students. In these situations, educators have several different options. We can choose to ignore the silence and move forward, as I did in the first example when I offered my own explanation for the silence, rather than waiting for a response and seeking to fully understand the student teachers' silence. Sometimes, this response is necessary because of the pressure to cover more material. Alternatively, educators can raise questions about the silence and analyze it individually with the student or with the whole class. We can craft individual or group solutions similar to my agreement with Alison. Or, taking the perspective that the silent class and the silent individual are products of classroom interactions, local norms, and a larger sociopolitical context, a teacher might choose to interrogate the silences in her classroom with the students themselves. This chapter addresses how a K–12 teacher or university instructor might engage in this kind of collaborative investigation.

As I have argued throughout the book, there is not a single meaning or correct response to student—or classroom—silences. Rather, there are multiple interpretations of and functions for silence in classrooms, several ways to teach through silence or to add openings in the form of silence to pedagogical practice, and a variety of tools to interrogate silence that draw on the understandings described in this book. I begin by reviewing the connotations of silence in classrooms developed throughout this book. An understanding of these meanings provides teachers with a basis to develop a broader perspective on the role of silence in teaching and learning and a blueprint for incorporating these ideas into classroom practice.

MEANINGS OF STUDENT SILENCE IN CLASSROOMS

In her poem, "The Cartographies of Silence," Adrienne Rich (1984) writes:

> Silence can be a plan
> rigorously executed
>
> the blueprint to a life
>
> It is a presence
> it has a history a form

Do not confuse it
with any kind of absence
(pp. 232–236)

This book takes a sociocultural perspective on silence. In other words, silence in classrooms is understood to be interactionally produced and shaped by broader sociocultural patterns in a particular historical moment and geographic location. As Rich explains, silence has a presence whether it is expressed through the absence of words or through other modalities. As such, I focus on *how* silence works in classrooms and how students are *produced* as silent (or talkative), rather than on individual students who are thought to *be* silent. At times, students are assumed to choose silence, although that choice is always informed by the models of how to be a student that are available to them (Wortham, 2006) and the possibilities for expressing themselves through the verbal and nonverbal channels they have in their classrooms, schools, and communities. For instance, Wortham (2006) writes about a student, William, who is predictably silent. He explains that William has claimed this social identity that is constructed in practice through his teacher's and peers' language and actions, such as when his teacher says, "We don't usually hear from William" (pp. 30–31). Wortham conjectures that there are many possible interpretations for William's silence, and that its meaning is determined by the local, circulating models of how to be a student in this classroom.

It is useful for teachers to explore a wide range of interpretations of classroom silences in order to be open to the various explanations for how and why students might enact silence. There are several paradoxical meanings of silence in classrooms that serve to illuminate the range of possibilities. For instance, there are engaged and disengaged silences, productive and unproductive ones. Some silences are appropriate to particular times and contexts. Silence can indicate deep respect and, conversely, it can be wielded as a sign of disrespect. Silences contain meanings intrinsic to communication; some silences are empty and pointless. Silences are most often chosen by students. On the other hand, students can be silenced by teachers, peers, and schools as institutions (Schultz, 2003). Basso (e.g., 1996) found that silence reflects cultural norms and is closely tied to ambiguous relationships. Yet many people experience the easy silence between intimates, suggesting that silence also accompanies familiarity. Two common, yet opposing, understandings of silence are as resistance or a refusal to participate and as compliance or silent assent. Silence can represent a presence in the classroom (Campano, 2007; Rich, 1984) and also an absence, leading a student to appear invisible. Silences also contain emotions. Sometimes, students participate through silence out of fear or anger. Other times, silence masks inexpressible joy or passion that may be inadmissible in a classroom.

Silence allows people to hold onto time and space for reflection and contemplation, using silence to retreat from conversation and interaction. When learning a new language or concept, silence can be used to create additional time and space for learning. While silence signals a chance to withdraw, silence can also signal a request for help from teachers or peers, as illustrated in Chapter 3. Silence is a container for painful memories, acting as protection and a means to guard secrets. Surrounding oneself in silence and responding in silence are two of the many ways that people draw boundaries around themselves. Sometimes, the boundary protects a student from ridicule; other times, it protects a person from the need to talk about what she deems unspeakable. Student silence might be a cause for concern (Burbules, 2004) or a practice that a teacher needs to learn to comprehend.

In addition to students' silence in classrooms, teachers use silence to inform their decision-making and pedagogical practice. Teachers integrate silence into their teaching and students' learning and develop routines that incorporate silence, sometimes breaking the silence to encourage more talk. Silence allows teachers to create openings in their classrooms and curriculum to invite more students to participate in activities. Teachers also seek silence as a form of control, alternatively worrying about times when there is too much silence. Silence organizes interactions in classrooms. Sometimes, this silence is orchestrated by teachers; other times, by students. Like Mattie Davis, teachers can use silence to communicate respect and give students authorial control of their writing and talk.

SILENCE, PARTICIPATION, AND DEMOCRATIC PRACTICE

Teachers have particular expectations of students in classrooms. In general, they expect students to be silent until they are called on, attending to the teacher's directions and instructions and to the contributions of their peers. They expect students to participate verbally in class discussions for a variety of reasons: to display their knowledge; complete written assignments, tests, and quizzes; and treat their teachers and peers with respect. This respect generally entails not only kind words, but also silence while others are speaking. Although many teachers establish classrooms where there is an expectation that students will talk and contribute, in general, teachers hope that students are compliant (obedient), engaged (active), and productive members of the classroom community (i.e., good citizens who are aware that they are one among many). The term *participation* captures all of these activities, although it is rarely specified as such.

118   RETHINKING CLASSROOM PARTICIPATION

Participation is a term that is often associated with democracy. As Torre and Fine (2006) explain, "Participation lies at the core of democracy and justice" (p. 269). Democratic schools and classrooms are generally characterized as places where students have access and opportunities to contribute to decisions related to their learning and where authority is shared. The relationship between silences and democratic practice became more clear to me in a 3-year research project that I conducted with colleagues in a racially balanced middle school (Schultz & Davis, 1996; Schultz, Buck, & Niesz, 2000). In this project, we sought to understand students' conceptions of race and racial relations at this juncture in history. Our analysis of conversations about race and race relations suggested the salience of what we termed *democratic conversations*, or interactions that invite multiple perspectives, including those perspectives that are privileged or silenced (Schultz, Buck, & Niesz, 2000, p. 33). We conceptualize democratic conversations as interactions that include conflict and improvisation rather than equal participation. The silences in the conversations between and among Black and White students prompted us to explore how to conduct such conversations, including the pitfalls and opportunities they present.

We learned that in order to engage in these democratic conversations, it was critical for students and teachers to work together to build a vocabulary and set of lenses with which to identify and explicate the silencing and misuses of power in the midst of talk. For instance, middle and high school teachers might guide students to develop means to communicate an understanding of power dynamics embedded within their conversation and reflected in the local sociohistorical and political context. In addition, they might work with students to develop an analysis of the institutional assumptions that shape their interactions. In such conversations, individuals are encouraged to articulate their perspectives and bring their identities into the conversation (Schultz, Buck, & Niesz, 2000). To return to the example in Chapter 2, when Luis entered the conversation about J. Edgar Hoover and the FBI in his high school classroom, he articulated a social analysis, contributing to the building conversation. In order to make local dynamics of classroom discussions more transparent, teachers can initiate conversations about their decisions.

In my own teacher education classes, I provide prospective teachers with multiple opportunities to lead and participate in literature groups when I teach them the practice of leading discussions. Our analyses of these experiences include a discussion of our own classroom dynamics, including the patterns of talk and silence. In one such conversation, a student teacher, Sharon, pointed out that in her role as discussion leader, she chose to provide a clear structure for turn-taking to the group. She elaborated that she often felt uncomfortable with more open-ended participation structures where students jump into conversations, interrupting one another. Sharon is a student who was noticeably quiet in whole-group discussions; she explained in this discussion, however, that she was simply more comfortable if she knew when it would be her turn to speak. Later, in response to a classmate's statement that Sharon typically chose to be silent in class, Sharon spoke up and explained that she knew she was often cast in the role as a silent student. After that interchange, Sharon became more talkative in that class, making new kinds of contributions to the class community. Although I do not suggest that conversations such as these are easy, they are critical for building and maintaining an inclusive, democratic practice.

The definition of participation in this book goes well beyond the ways that participation is typically understood and used in schools. Participation, as I have argued throughout this book, is much more than showing up or contributing a verbal statement to a conversation. At times, silence is a form of participation. Importantly, we can explore *what* a person contributes to a conversation or a classroom as well as *how* he participates. If the contribution is verbose, yet only tangentially related to the topic, it may be less important than the short statement or gesture that shifts the direction of the discussion and illuminates the learning or a statement that comes after silence and reflection. The notion of building democratic practice hinges on reframing classroom participation as engaged participation whether verbal or silent, through auditory or visual modes.

Anderson (1998) explains how the language of participation is connected to ideals of democracy, writing:

> Drawing on Dewey's (1944) notion of democratic community, participatory democrats argue that the future of democracy depends on the existence of local social spaces in which human actors can learn and exercise the skills of dialogue and debate necessary for the development of a democratic citizenry. (p. 575)

Historically, one of the purposes of schools in the United States has been to educate an informed citizenry who can take an active role in our democracy (Labaree, 1997). In a global society, schools must address the needs and knowledge of youth who are simultaneously members of both global and local communities (Schultz, Vasudevan, & Throop, 2007). This suggests the importance of taking into account our increasingly diverse school populations and the growing access that youth have to new technologies and global practices outside of school. The changing nature of schooling suggests the need to redefine what we mean by the role of participation in schools. Darling-Hammond (1996) argues that we need not only to have education *for* democracy or education that prepares students as engaged citizens, with skills for the next century, but also education *as* democracy, or "education that gives students access to social understanding developed by actually participating in a pluralistic community by talking and making decisions with one another and coming to understand multiple perspectives" (p. 6).

Listening for, inquiring into, and honoring silence might lead to louder, more dynamic, and engaged classrooms that have moments of stillness where students pause for reflection. Most importantly, inquiry into classroom silence and participation might lead to classrooms where equitable participation is defined as broadly as possible. Educators can learn to listen to these silences, to provide possibilities both for translating the silences into speech and allowing students to use silence productively. This includes understanding how and when children (and adults) might choose to remain silent. Understanding the role of silence in teaching and learning has the potential to allow us to notice and understand more about current classroom dynamics and re-imagine classroom practices in the future.

INVESTIGATING SILENCE BY TAKING AN INQUIRY STANCE

Without understanding students' uses of silence in the classroom, teachers risk missing much of the participation and learning that transpires. A language for interpreting silence allows teachers to understand how students contribute to classroom discourse in a variety of ways, including through nonverbal modalities. If teachers rely only on written answers to test questions or on verbal responses to ascertain students' learning, they have limited access to what students know and narrow ways to include them in the classroom community. Further, if there are no explicit discussions about the role and importance of talk and silence and the multiple ways to enact these forms of communication, including multiple modalities, students are left with few ways to participate in classroom discussions and classroom life more broadly.

There are several ways a teacher might initiate an investigation into the silences and nature of participation in his classroom. The inquiry might focus on a particular event (e.g., a time in the classroom where there was notable silence that the class can investigate together), a pattern that the teacher has noticed (certain times of the day or week when there is more silence than talk or groups of students who tend to be silent at certain times), or a more general exploration. It should be emphasized that I do not advocate the exploration of silence to eliminate it from classrooms or from a student's repertoire of responses. Instead, I argue that silence, like talk, is a key component of classroom interaction that can be usefully explored by teachers and students to understand more about the norms and practices in a classroom, making them transparent. Classrooms are complicated places where students' and teachers' roles and identities are in constant flux. An awareness of the possible interpretations and uses of talk and silence and an investigation of these modalities together allows a teacher to respond to classroom conditions and to see and hear more of the learning that transpires. Understanding that talk and silence are continuous and deeply intertwined suggests that teachers see conditions of silence as leading to talk and, conversely, talk as a condition that engenders silence.

There is silence in every classroom. Often, the silence is interlaced with talk. Always, it is filled with meaning. We tend to privilege talk in the classroom, assuming, like Amelia Coleman, that if a person is not talking, she is not engaged in learning. An exploration of the local meanings of silence reveals how and whether students in a classroom are learning through silence. The study of the emic or insider's perspectives of silence in relationship to talk can illuminate and make public the understandings held by teachers and students. This can be done through taking an inquiry stance, which is defined by Cochran-Smith and Lytle (1999) as follows:

> *Inquiry as stance* as a construct for understanding teacher learning in communities relies on a richer conception of knowledge than that allowed by the traditional formal knowledge–practical knowledge distinction, a richer conception of practice than that suggested in the aphorism that practice is practical, a richer conception of learning across the professional life span than concepts of expertise that differentiate expert teachers from novices, and a richer conception of the cultures of communities and educational purposes than those implicit in many widespread school-wide reforms. (p. 289)

Building on the above argument, I suggest that teachers and students collaboratively take an inquiry stance toward silence in classrooms to understand how silence works, including an exploration of the conditions that promote silence and those that promote talk. As Cochran-Smith and Lytle (1999) explain, this stance focuses not only on the practical, or how to shift teacher and student practices to address silence, nor solely on the theoretical or the multiple constructs for noticing and making sense of silence. One approach for exploring how silence works in the classroom is for teachers and students to engage in collaborative inquiry into conditions that foster silence and those that support talk, keeping in mind that the choice to talk or remain silent is often both an individual decision and one guided by the local sociopolitical context of the classroom, the school, and society at large in a particular moment in time.

Taking an inquiry stance toward silence in the classroom suggests that silence—and talk—is conceptualized as a phenomenon to be studied rather than a characteristic of an individual or even a group. This stance incorporates an exploration of practices and the meanings of those practices to the teachers and students. In addition, it includes an investigation of the sociopolitical context that shapes local practices. Taking an inquiry stance toward silence suggests an ongoing investigation into the relationship between silence and talk, rather than a bounded study of this phenomenon and an emphasis on *how* silence works rather than *who* is silent. It suggests that this is a topic that teachers and students address together in the daily course of classroom interaction.

It is useful, however, to consider some of the questions from throughout this book that a teacher might usefully address through taking an inquiry stance on a particular issue. The following questions, among others, might guide teachers to pursue projects around single questions or they might serve as springboards for teachers interested in pursuing a larger inquiry project around talk and silence in their classrooms:

How does silence work in the classroom?

- What is the relationship between talk and silence in this classroom? What are the varying amounts of talk and silence? How do they interact with one another? What is the quality of silence and of talk in the classroom?
- What are the relationships between individual silences and group silences? What are the topics around which people are silent? Which topics engender talk?
- What are the norms for participation? When is silence a group norm and when is it an individual decision?
- What kinds of participation do various forms of silence indicate?

What are the functions and understandings of silence in the classroom?

- How is silence used in the classroom by teachers and by students? In the classroom, who talks and who remains silent? How does this vary? When does silence occur? When is silence silenced and when are students expected to talk? Are there times when it is acceptable (or even preferable) to be silent, and are there times when silence is not allowed? What is the relationship of talk to silence? For instance, is there more time allocated to silence or talk during particular periods during the day?

- How is silence connected to power in the classroom? Who controls silence? Who controls talk? Are silence and talk used to assert power or claim space?
- What are the various understandings and explanations by teachers and students of their silences? What does silence indicate?

What are some possible responses to student silences?

- When should teachers interrogate an individual student's silence, and when is it important simply to support that student to participate through silence? How can teachers tell the difference between an engaged and a disengaged silence?
- How much responsibility to the group does the individual have to participate verbally in classroom interactions? When should teachers accept silence and when should they create conditions that promote speech so that students are a part of the public discourse?
- When are silences acceptable (or necessary) as a form of participation, and when do they foreclose learning (for the individual or for the group)? When does silence promote learning, and when does it signal retreat or disengagement?

This list is meant to be suggestive rather than exhaustive. A teacher is not likely to investigate all of these questions in her classroom with students. The decision about which questions to investigate depends on the age of the students, the interests of the teachers and students, the ways that silence works in the particular classroom, and the transparency of silence in the classroom. It is often useful for teachers to begin with a nagging question that is closely tied to the problems or challenges they identify in their own classroom practice. For instance, most teachers worry about student engagement, which is typically linked to classroom participation and focused only on verbal contributions. This suggests questions such as: Who participates or engages in learning on a typical day during specific activities? Who is not engaged and why not? What does the lack of participation (sometimes read as silence) mean? These straightforward and common questions can lead to powerful inquiry projects or action research projects conducted by teachers and students about questions that are immediately relevant to their context, often leading to changes in the classroom environment. Teachers and students might begin with the questions that arise out of their own experiences in schools, such as: How do silence and talk work together? These questions represent a starting place for ongoing investigations into silence and talk in classrooms. Rather than assuming the primacy of talk in the classroom, taking an inquiry stance toward both silence and talk suggests making the uses of silence in teaching and learning a subject for ongoing study and interrogation.

Taking an inquiry stance suggests that the practice of raising questions and noticing patterns can be integrated into the daily conversations and patterns of classroom interactions. For instance, during or after a discussion in which there has been noticeable silence, a teacher might habitually ask the class, "What did you notice about this discussion?" She might begin by asking students to write about their participation in the discussion and the roles they each took. It is critical to emphasize to students (and teachers) that some conversations are going to be uncomfortable and that, at times, discomfort is necessary in order for learning to transpire. Asking students to reflect on their roles in discussions and in teaching and learning activities emphasizes the expectation of engaged participation.

As Cochran-Smith and Lytle (1999) explain, taking an inquiry stance implies positioning oneself in relation to the context and suggests a particular perspective. It implies embracing a state of not knowing or uncertainty and a commitment to learning and investigation. I suggest that when teachers invite students to take an inquiry stance about the role of silence and talk in participation, they open up dialogue about the meanings of silence and the ways that silence and talk work in the classroom. This can lead to ongoing conversations about how teaching and learning occur, the nature of participation, and how to leave openings for new voices, new stories, and new perspectives. In addition to taking a stance that opens up everyday conversations about silence and talk, there are a few tools that teachers can use to interrogate silence in their classrooms.

TOOLS FOR UNDERSTANDING STUDENT SILENCE

The most important tools for interrogating silence in a classroom are listening carefully and observing interaction to identify patterns. Beyond these strategies, I introduce a few tools that can be used to uncover local meanings, functions, and uses of silence and talk. Although this can be a project for a teacher or group of teachers in an inquiry group, I encourage teachers to investigate and interrogate the silences in their classroom in collaboration with their students when possible. It is often difficult for teachers to find time to engage in research, either because of the pressure of mandated curriculum or because their time is filled with demands from multiple parties, including parents, administrators, and children. Joining with colleagues in an inquiry group to investigate practice is often an important source of support for this kind of work.

Holding Classroom Discussions

Teachers and students can develop procedures for using moments that arise in the course of teaching as an opportunity to investigate silence and talk. For instance, Rymes (2008) reports the following dialogue in a second-grade reading group engaged in a discussion about a picture book:

> SALLY: (*pointing to a picture in the book*) They're White and every-body else is Black.
> TEACHER: Oh, so her friend is White and everybody else is Black in the picture?
> DANNY: Hey don't you be talking about that.
> TEACHER: What is wrong with that?
> DANNY: Nothing. (*Danny shakes his head*)
> SALLY: Nothing.
> TEACHER: Is there anything wrong with that?
> STUDENTS: No. (*Sally shakes her head*)
> TEACHER: No, I didn't think so either. (adapted from pp. 274–275)

Although the children in this class were young, with practice and tools, the teacher could have used this moment to explore what Danny meant by his initial comment, "Hey don't you be talking about that", which shut down the conversation about race among these students, replacing talk with silence. It should be noted that Danny was the only African American boy in a group of White children. His teacher was also White. A teacher might feel more comfortable returning to the topic later with the group, rather than addressing it in the moment. It might also be useful for this teacher to invite Danny to discuss his reasons for avoiding the topic of race at a separate time, exploring his reasons for believing it was not an appropriate conversation for his reading group, or perhaps for school. It may be that his parents instructed him not to talk about race in school. Without putting Danny on the spot, at a later time with the whole class, the teacher could inquire into the students' rush to silence around this topic, asking questions such as: What topics did we talk about in our discussion about the book? What topics did we avoid talking about? Why do you think we avoided those topics? If you were to talk about them, what might you say? In the moment, the teacher might have opened up the conversation, at least briefly, by asking Danny, "What do you mean by that? Are there other topics we shouldn't talk about? Are there times when it is okay to talk about these topics?" She could have encouraged the whole group to join the conversation so that Danny was not the focus of attention, making sure that Danny had the opportunity to speak if he so desired. Discussion in an inquiry group or with colleagues might lead the teacher to feel more comfortable raising these questions and extending these conversations.

Similar questions can be explored in high school and university class-rooms. For instance, prospective teachers sometimes make disparaging comments about the low-income, often less-educated parents of their students in my own teacher education classroom located in an urban context. Recently, in a colleague's class, a student said, "Because the students come from homes where the parents cannot help them with homework and don't care, we need to use these kinds of practices." When I hear this type of comment, I always need to decide whether to interrupt the student, weighing the risk of shutting down the conversation and the participation of this particular student with the risk of colluding with a stereotypical statement. Usually, I simply say something like, "I've never met a parent who didn't want the best for her child." That kind of response serves to establish parameters of how we talk about children from my perspective, but does not confront and address the assumptions that are implicit in the statement. In the moment, I have to balance the need to maintain the flow of the conversation with the importance of unpacking a statement; later, I can address these issues more comprehensively. Each time, I make a different decision.

It is critical for students of all ages and their teachers to have practice in holding conversations that may lead to silence. The earlier example illustrates how useful it is for teachers of young children—as well as high school and university teachers—to be prepared to respond to student questions and observations about difficult or potentially controversial topics. If Danny's class had never had any practice engaging in conversations about race and racism and other complex issues, it may have been too difficult for them to participate in such a discussion and for their teacher to open up the topic. It is important not to put single members of an identity category in the position of speaking for their group or educating others. An exploration of silence and talk suggests that educators pay attention to who talks and who is silent, and the nature of the participation of students and the teacher through both talk and silence. In addition, it is useful for teachers to consider which conversations are admissible and the conditions that allow students to participate through talk and silence.

There are several ways a teacher might initiate a discussion about classroom silence. As suggested at the beginning of the chapter, teachers might choose to hold whole-class discussions about silence as a way to establish classroom norms or in response to a particular classroom situation that involves ubiquitous silence (or talk) by individuals or the group. Alternatively, a teacher might initiate such a discussion with an individual student through conversation or a written dialogue, similar to my email correspondence with Alison. There are several ways to begin a discussion about silence—whether it is a group or individual conversation—and these methods always depend on the context, time of year, and the individual students and teachers involved in the conversation. While some teachers might simply want to brainstorm what silence looks and feels like in a classroom, others might opt to begin with a more concrete activity that is easier for students to embrace. For instance, a teacher might begin with a discussion of an occurrence of silence in the classroom. This might be a real or a fictional event. Students can be asked to describe a time when there was silence, to write what it looked, sounded, and felt like. This could lead to a discussion about participation and what participation looks like during and through silence. Beginning with a time when there was silence in the classroom emphasizes the social nature of silence rather than a focus on silence as connected only to individuals.

On the other hand, a teacher can ask students to write or draw a portrait of a student who typically enacts silence as a prelude to a variety of conversations. The portrait might be fictional or it might be based on a real individual. It is useful for the teachers to establish clear parameters around assignments such as this one. For instance, it may be important for the teacher to state that the portrait should not be of an individual in the classroom, in order to create a safe enough environment for an open discussion. The teacher can then ask the students to respond to simple questions such as when and why the person is silent and, conversely, when and why that person is talkative. It may be useful to begin by reading published portraits or biographical (or autobiographical) sketches of individuals who were marked or cast as silent, such as Kingston's (1989) *Woman Warrior*. Alternatively, teachers might introduce film or television clips that illustrate silence and silencing as a prompt for class discussion about their own classroom dynamics. This kind of activity can lead to the generation of lists of what silence looks like in a classroom, how students enact silence, and what events or activities might lead a student (or group of students) to enact a silent stance. A teacher can help to frame this discussion in terms of understanding how students might choose to take on a silent stance in the local context of the classroom community. Beginning with some of the conceptualizations of silence explored in this book, a teacher can help students elaborate their own ideas.

One reason for the public investigation of these ideas with students is to establish parameters for participation in the classroom and to make the norms for talk and silence clear and explicit. In order to democratize classrooms, it is useful for teachers to make their expectations transparent and accessible to all students. This might begin with the teacher's exploration of her own assumptions about how and where learning occurs and the acceptable ways for demonstrating the acquisition of knowledge. Furthermore, an examination of who makes these decisions is critical. For instance, a teacher might ask herself whether students can participate through silence in the classroom. If so, what does that look like and when can it happen? After students develop descriptions of a silent event or portraits of students enacting silence and teachers gather ideas about silence, the next step is to connect this discussion to the actual classroom. Rather than singling out individual students who may choose silence, this activity can lead to a discussion about what the teacher expects in terms of talk and silence in the classroom:

- Does the teacher believe that learning is reflected in talk? Are there ways in this classroom to show engagement and participation through silence?
- How can learning and engagement be made visible for the teacher and other members of the classroom community? What are the assumptions about silence that students bring to the classroom?
- Where do these assumptions come from?
- What are the teacher's assumptions?

Once there is a list of what silence and the enactment of silence look and sound like in a particular classroom, the participants can address the following questions:

- How do the teacher and the students accommodate silence, and what are the norms that support silent interactions?
- What are the relationships between silence and talk in the classroom?
- How can the teacher incorporate silence into these discussions?
- What modalities might be introduced in place of talk to give students new entry points into the conversation?
- How can silence be conceptualized as produced through classroom interactions rather than as an attribute of an individual?

Concrete descriptions of silence can be a helpful starting place for such discussions. These discussions might occur between the teacher and students and among students initially or throughout the year to allow understandings and possibilities for participation to be continually negotiated and renegotiated.

Analyzing Records of Classroom Conversations

The analysis of how talk and silence work in a classroom is most usefully tied to real rather than hypothetical examples. For instance, conversations can be recorded in writing or through audio and/or video recorders. Although this might seem difficult for teachers to manage, if there are student teachers or assistants in the classroom, or if there is the support of an inquiry group of colleagues, the task might seem more manageable. Rymes (2008) provides clear instructions for teachers to record, transcribe, and analyze talk in their classrooms. I encourage teachers to involve students in the process of making sense of the transcribed data that they collect, with a particular eye toward understanding how talk and silence function in the classroom.

For instance, in a transcript of talk, the teacher and/or students might determine the nature of participation in the conversation. This includes an investigation of who talks and who is silent. Together, they might examine whether and how students have participated through silence and what this participation looks like. Periods of silence can be noted through counting seconds. Transcripts of classroom talk are also productive sites for understanding the role of silence in classroom discourse. Together, teachers and students might interrogate the patterns of talk and silence, raising questions about why there are silences and the meanings behind them:

- Is there a predictable pattern of talk and silence?
- Are there particular kinds of questions or topics that engender silence? That produce talk?
- Are there particular speakers who are typically followed by silence or talk?

The transcript presented in Chapter 3 is a good example of the kind of transcript that might be used in these conversations. (See the Appendix for a complete transcript of the event.)

Transcripts allow for a close look at the patterns of talk and silence. It may also be useful to videotape a classroom and explore that videotape with the students themselves. This can be done with both younger and older students. Students and teachers can watch a videotape of classroom interaction to prompt a general conversation about talk and silence in the classroom. Teachers might initiate a conversation about the classroom dynamics by asking an open-ended question such as: What do you notice or what is going on here? As students learn how to notice, listen, and watch interaction, the questions can be refined. It takes practice to develop the necessary language and lenses for observation. In the beginning, this talk among students may need to be scaffolded. With practice, students of all ages can use an ethnographic lens to understand what is happening in their classrooms. For instance, ethnographic research in education focuses on what group members need to know, do, predict, and interpret in order to participate in everyday life within their social groups or com-munities, which include classrooms and schools (Heath, 1982). These basic ethnographic questions can help teachers and students uncover taken-for-granted patterns of interaction in classrooms, making visible the otherwise hidden norms of behavior.

Teachers and students can also make notations of who speaks and who is silent in videotapes of classroom interactions by noting the patterns of talk. For instance, Cazden (2001; see also Rymes, 2008) suggests using the simple notations of T and S for "teacher" and "student" (and S1, S2, etc., for various students) to indicate turns and illuminate who dominates class-room discourse. For instance, in a teacher-dominated classroom, the no-tation might look like this:

TTTTTTS1TTS2TTS3TTTTTTTT.

Alternatively, the notation for a student-led activity like the Author's Chair, described in Chapter 3, might look like this:

TS1TS2S3S3S4S4S3S3S5S6S3S3 and so on.

The difference between the two patterns of interaction is stark. These notations only display the patterns of talk. It would take further investi-gation to determine, over the course of a certain period of time, who is talking and who is silent and what kinds of participation occurred through the silence of the teacher and students. A more sophisticated analysis might indicate silent participation with brackets in addition to the talk, such as:

T[S1][T][S1]T[T][S1]S2T[S1]S3.

Making the patterns of participation of talk and silence visible opens up the possibilities for discussion.

Re-enacting Scenes of Classroom Interactions

Rymes (2008; see also Rymes, Cahnmann-Taylor, & Souto-Manning, 2008) writes about the possibilities of using techniques developed by Boal (2000, 2002) to work with educators to understand various perspectives on class-room life. Boal has developed methods for drawing the audience into the performance, breaking the artificial barrier between actor and audience or spectator (reframing them as the "spectACTor"), using the new partici-pants to enact or revisit scenes of oppression. Rymes (2008) suggests adapt-ing this technique to work with teachers and students, inviting them to take on different roles in transcripts of classroom conversations to gain new per-spectives and understandings of what has transpired. This technique is par-ticularly effective to remake classroom scenes that are disquieting (Rymes, 2008; Rymes, Cahnmann-Taylor, & Souto-Manning, 2008).

For instance, Rymes (2008) suggests that a group of teachers can re-enact a scene where there is an impasse. Likewise, a teacher can record and transcribe a particularly charged interaction among students and ask the students to take on the role of a peer in order to understand a differ-ent point of view and possibly work through the barriers to understand-ing. Working together, teachers and students can adapt this same technique to investigate talk and silence in their classrooms. Taking on new class-room roles—e.g., the roles of more talkative and more silent students, or switching teacher and student roles—could give participants a greater understanding of the various roles they play in the classroom. As Rymes (2008) explains:

> I cannot predict what resources students would draw on as they re-visited a scene like this. However, I can guarantee that spectacting this scene would be a powerful way to extend the dialogue. Re-doing scenes like these is poten-tially as liberating for students as it may be for teachers. And, after some prac-tice enacting multiple possibilities, students, like teachers, may wake up the next morning, able to try out new ways of talking, listening, and acting in class and in the world. Because, after the redoing, comes the revisiting. (p. 345)

Enacting democratizing conversations includes attempts to understand and take on multiple perspectives while tracing the ways power works in class-room interactions. Taking on different roles allows for the possibilities of new conversations and understandings of the role of silence as participa-tion. The use of transcripts for this process keeps the activity tied to actual classroom practice and makes it less likely that students will stereotype or tease one another. The point of this activity with respect to talk and si-lence is to build understandings of the various ways that both talk and silence constitute participation in classrooms. This kind of activity builds understanding through experiencing other ways of being or participating in a classroom.

Providing Opportunities for Talk and Silence

Although the emphasis of this chapter is on the collaborative exploration and interrogation of silence and talk, there may be times when a teacher might decide to explore classroom silences on his own. In Chapter 2, I describe several teachers who responded with patience to students who took on a silent stance, allowing the individuals to have the time and space to decide when and how to talk and contribute to conversations. In each of these instances, the students began to speak when they had something that was critically important to say. This suggests that teachers consider how often they provide students with these authentic moments for speech in schools. There is no tool or technique for teachers to learn the patience needed to let a student remain silent for months at a time. At the same time, a teacher has to be aware of when students are quiet without contributing to the classroom learning community. Teachers need to be careful not to let students opt out of participation, while at the same time supporting them to remain silent if that silence is a form of participation that may lead to verbal engagement or participation in another modality.

At times, students who were otherwise silent contributed to a class discussion through other modalities in activities such as the multimodal storytelling project in Amelia Coleman's fifth-grade classroom. As educators, we can ask ourselves how often we provide opportunities for students to talk about and act on topics that feel vital or deeply connected to their lives. Do we provide them with alternative pathways for expression? On the other hand, in contrast to students who appear silent in classrooms, casting themselves in that particular role, there are always students who are disengaged from learning and manifest this condition through talk rather than silence. In other words, neither talk nor silence should be a proxy for participation and disengagement.

CURRICULAR INNOVATIONS
TO RETHINK PARTICIPATION

There are several ways that educators have created spaces for students who may be silent to participate, including the introduction of popular culture into classrooms, Youth Participatory Action Research or opportunities for youth to investigate and respond to community problems, the incorporation of community funds of knowledge into the curriculum, and the integration of knowledge from out of school arts-based organizations into the school curriculum. The following examples, which are meant to be illustrative rather than exhaustive, describe curricular innovations that address student silence through increasing their participation in and out of school. Importantly, each of these curricular practices suggests how curricular content and pedagogical practices can be brought together and adapted to bring students' interests and knowledge into classrooms, reflecting possibilities for addressing student silence. Taken together, they suggest new possibilities for participation and rethinking the meanings of silence in classroom learning.

Popular Culture and the Classroom Curriculum

Ms. Coleman drew frequently on popular culture to attract students' attention and make topics such as grammar more enjoyable. Teachers might also use popular culture and new media as a means to build on students' knowledge and provide them with alternative entry points into the curriculum. Bridging youth-oriented popular culture and media with the more formal school curriculum provides the possibility of increasing student engagement in learning (Schultz & Throop, in press). For instance, as Dyson (e.g., 2003) demonstrates, youth's knowledge, familiarity, and use of popular culture can reshape the official school curriculum and the teaching of writing. Through their use of compelling images and ideas from popular culture texts, including the incorporation of familiar characters and plotlines, Dyson illustrates how young children can transform the school curriculum through writing, talk, and play. When teachers allow children to bring popular culture into their writing, the nature of learning and writing is changed. Popular culture can provide an avenue for student engagement with school curriculum, suggesting the erasure of the formal boundaries between in- and out-of-school contexts (Hull & Schultz, 2002). We designed the multimodal storytelling projects described in Chapter 4 to provide opportunities for youth to bring their home knowledge into school and to recognize that knowledge along with the texts produced and collected outside of school. Creating boundaries between home and school often reinforces silences, marking what can and cannot be said and written at school. A teacher's decision to incorporate popular culture into the classroom can blur these boundaries and provide additional resources and opportunities for learning.

Youth Participatory Action Research

Recently, there has been increasing interest in Youth Participatory Action Research (YPAR), a curricular approach that invites youth to study social problems that affect their lives, constructing responses and solutions to address these problems (e.g., Cammarota & Fine, 2008; McIntyre, 2000). In YPAR, young people research issues, investigate how power and oppression work, and develop ways to speak back to and challenge conditions of injustice through critical inquiry and action. As Fine and her colleagues (2007) explain, through the praxis of the melding of research and action (e.g., Freire, 1970), YPAR allows youth to move "beyond silence in a quest to proclaim the world" (p. 808). For example, Fine and her colleagues describe their project, *Echoes of Brown* (e.g., Fine, Roberts, & Torre, 2004), which combined artistic performances with research, bringing together youth and adults from a range of backgrounds to analyze patterns of social injustice related to what they term the *opportunity gap*. This project allowed youth to connect personal and historical struggles, investigate critical issues that they identified, and represent their findings in a variety of ways through public performances. These performances allow teachers to evaluate students' learning and, importantly, to educate others as a form of action. The following vignette illustrates the types of conversations and learning engendered by this project. Although it occurred outside of a school context, many aspects of this work could be integrated into classroom research projects.

> Youth and adults involved in the *Echoes of Brown* project were gathered to listen to a speaker with expertise in civil rights issues. After a heated discussion about desegregation and specifically about the desirability of a separate school for LGBTQ youth, a young man spoke for the first time in this group about the pain he had experienced from being separated and labeled as a special education student: "That's why I said [in my poem] that the silence is just as painful, because like no one, honestly, *no one's* speaking about it. And that's what's killing us." The young man went on to say that as a result of this project he had learned that he needed to speak up in order to consider himself an activist. He explained that through his spoken word poetry he would bear witness and speak for himself and the millions of others labeled as "special education" students. (Torre & Fine et al., 2008)

Youth Participatory Action Research is a pedagogical practice that provides opportunities for youth to participate in learning that is directly tied to action both in and out of school. Like multimodal storytelling, this process opens up possibilities for participation that may not ordinarily be available for some students, allowing them to translate silence into public performance. In schools, some teachers find ways to incorporate this research and action into mandated social studies topics and community service requirements. Providing youth with tools to research and speak out about issues that directly affect their lives offers authentic reasons to take a public stance that reflects considerable learning and translates the experience of being silenced into talk and action.

Community Funds of Knowledge

In another example of a research-based stance on teaching and learning that connects school and community worlds, González, Moll, and Amanti (2005) describe their work with community "funds of knowledge" in a Mexican American community, illustrating how teachers can draw on the expertise of parents and community members to develop curricula (cf., Moll, 1992;

Moll & Greenberg, 1990). Through this focus, teachers learn about the every-day routines of family lives through a series of ethnographic interviews and observations. As González, Moll, and Amanti (2005) explain:

> Funds of knowledge are generated through the social and labor history of families and communicated to others through the activities that constitute household life, including through the formation of social networks that are central to any household's functioning within its particular environment. (p. 18)

Through their interviews with families, participating teachers found that children in households were active participants rather than passive and silent, behaviors they often displayed in school. In contrast to their unde-manding roles in school, youth were often required to participate actively in the running of households. Two teachers observed a boy selling Mexi-can candy in his neighborhood and used that event to develop an inte-grated curricular project that began with a research question posed by the students and ultimately involved science, math, social studies, and lan-guage arts. Parents and community members were invited into the class-room to share their expertise (see also Strieb, in preparation). In classrooms that draw on community funds of knowledge, the artificial boundary be-tween home and school is broken down so that students can draw on knowledge from a variety of contexts to learn in each of the settings. A shift in the curriculum in this direction can transform opportunities for student participation. Knowledge of students' homes and communities can enable teachers to change the structure and content of the curriculum to build on the resources that youth bring to school.

In our teacher education program at the University of Pennsylvania, new teachers are introduced to this stance in their initial summer courses through neighborhood studies of the community that surrounds the schools where the prospective teachers will work in the fall. Drawing on knowl-edge gained through neighborhood tours, interviews, and observations in the community, new teachers identify funds of knowledge and trends that they later incorporate into a rationale for a social studies curriculum unit. In order to counter the deficit perspectives that are common among pro-spective teachers, the instructors ask the future teachers to learn about the resources, assets, and strengths of the families, communities, and the students themselves (Buck & Skilton-Sylvester, 2005). In this assignment and throughout the program, the prospective teachers are taught to listen deeply to their students. As I explain (Schultz, 2003):

> The phrase "listening to teach" implies that the knowledge of who the learner is, and the understandings that both the teacher and learner bring to a

situation constitute the starting place for teaching. Listening encompasses written words as well as those that are spoken, words that are whispered, those enacted in gesture, and those left unsaid. It is an active process that allows us to both maintain and cross boundaries. (p. 13)

Learning to teach is a complicated process. In the program at Penn, part of the task of teacher preparation is to help new teachers learn how to learn from their students so that their pedagogy and curriculum can incorporate and respond to the students' cultural knowledge and their academic and social strengths and needs (Ball & Cohen, 1999; Schultz, Jones-Walker, & Chikkatur, 2008).

Arts-Based Organizations

Drawing on her research on community arts-based organizations, Heath (1998) writes about the collaborative teaching and learning that occurs as youth use their own knowledge and strategies in participatory projects. She explains that a curriculum or program based on the arts allows for new discourses that contribute to students' abilities to develop explanations, a critical aspect of learning. For instance, when students collaboratively write play scripts, plan and paint murals, or compose music, they have new opportunities for participation and learning that are not solely dependent on verbal contributions or modalities (Heath, 2000). Heath envisions schools as an integrated system of learning environments or "central nodes" within a web of learning contexts for children that might include museums, playgrounds, libraries, and other institutions that are open all day and all year. As she explains, "An ecology of learning environments would be the focus, rather than schools alone. In this way, societal members would reconceive young people as learners and resources for the learning of others rather than as passive students" (Heath, 2000, p. 128). Examples of projects in and out of school are useful for re-imagining classroom interactions to include a wider group of students and a broader array of participation strategies in classrooms. Teachers can attempt new curriculum projects; they can also find ways to reflect on their practices and understandings of silence and participation.

RESPONDING TO STUDENT SILENCE

The projects described above suggest ways to infuse new kinds of opportunities to draw students into participation and learning. In addition, it seems important for a teacher who allows students extra time to decide whether or not to participate to ascertain the level of engagement of those students who enact silence. The teacher may need to learn to read the silences or understand how the silences work in the landscape of the classroom. This is what Gallas (1998) did with the young student who remained silent for most of the year until she had an urgent story to tell, as I report in Chapter 2. It may be essential for some students to remain silent and for their teachers to work with them to accommodate this mode of class participation.

Also in Chapter 2, I elaborate how Campano (2007) established a separate, informal space for students to talk before school and during lunch. Shifting participation structures to create what he called a "second classroom" meant that one student who was typically silent became comfortable enough to speak in class and write her life story. Teachers can consider variations on this practice, especially if there is more than one student who appears silent in a classroom. Shifting participation structures to include individual writing, small groups, and work in pairs (sometimes called "think, pair, share") is a good way to draw more students into verbal participation in a class discussion. It also may be useful to create various informal spaces led either by the teacher—as Campano (2007) describes—or by the students themselves. These spaces might be built around activities such as storytelling; research; activist projects based on students' deep interests; explorations with multimodalities, as described in Chapter 4; and informal conversations. The point is not to replace silence with talk, but rather to give students a variety of venues for participation through silence *and* talk. Importantly, through close work, inquiry, and study with the students themselves, we can learn from them about how to create spaces and times for talk and silence, leading to more democratic and participatory classrooms.

The teacher might want to directly address this question with the student herself—as I did with Alison—in a dyadic manner that does not initially involve the rest of the class. Drawing on the research and findings in this book, there is a set of questions that a teacher might ask herself when there is a persistently silent student in her class. First, I suggest that a teacher look to the whole classroom and contextualize the silence in the sociocultural patterns of classroom talk:

- What are the conditions that promote silence for this student and support others to talk?
- What are some possible functions of the student's silence for the class as a whole? For herself? How is the role of "silent student" connected with other roles, such as one of compliance or disaffection?
- What other roles and identities can a typically silent student chose to enact, and what resources are necessary for this to happen?

- How are these roles and identities constructed for a student by the classroom community as a whole?
- What advantages seem to accrue to the student through this identity? What disadvantages?
- What are other available identities, and how do they interact?

More specifically, the teacher might ask herself, and possibly the student, what kinds of silence (or silences) characterize the student's participation in the class? For instance, is it an engaged or a disengaged silence? If the student is engaged, is she contributing to the classroom discourse in ways that are visible, if not audible?

If the student is silent because she is disengaged, then the teacher might examine his own teaching and the classroom dynamics to look for ways to draw the student into the classroom conversations through talk. This might include looking at one's own pedagogical practices as well as the content of the curriculum. In addition to a focus on his own practice, a teacher can work with the student to learn how to engage her in the class by looking for ways that the content might matter to the student and specific roles that the student might play in the classroom. If the student is engaged, yet silent, the teacher might simply work out a way for the student to stay in touch with the teacher through other modes than verbal participation, such as writing notes, meeting with the teacher to talk on an individual basis, talking regularly with a peer, or expressing ideas in another modality. The student's contributions through silence can be framed in relation to the larger set of social interactions in the classroom.

Rather than a focus on why the student is silent, the teacher can find a way to engage a student in a conversation around questions such as: What are the ways that you see yourself as involved through silence in the classroom? What might it take for you to become more vocally involved in the classroom? Sometimes, it is not a good idea for a teacher to pose these kind of questions directly to a student, because such a conversation might be threatening or uncomfortable, exacerbating the situation. A teacher would need to gauge his relationship with the student and determine whether there was enough trust for such a conversation. Rather than making a judgment about the lack of verbal participation, the teacher and student can develop an understanding about the nature of her participation in relation to the whole class. At some point, this might be a whole-class conversation. These reflective questions are directly tied to notions of democratic practices and understandings of what it means to have an inclusive classroom.

A teacher might raise questions about her own teaching, noticing if there are pedagogical practices that support some students to participate through talk and others through silence. If there are individuals or groups of students who are habitually silent, a teacher might ask herself whether there are ways to shift her practice to draw the voices of these students into the classroom conversation in a range of ways. For instance, I try to include a time where every student contributes her voice to the classroom conversation in my university classes. My hope is that giving everyone the time and space to speak might encourage students who are otherwise reluctant to participate through speaking aloud the practice and courage that they need to add verbally to the conversation. For example, I sometimes ask each student to respond in a sentence to a topic connected to the content of a particular class. I might ask for one-sentence responses to a book, article, or students' own writing, or instruct students to read aloud a line or quote from their own writing or the course text that stood out to them. As another example, before introducing a project to write a children's book, I prompt students to describe their favorite book from their childhood. For these particular structures, we simply go around the circle and each person is expected to contribute a phrase or a few sentences without cross-dialogue so that everyone has the opportunity to speak. Sometimes, I ask the students to write before we hold a conversation so that they can gather their thoughts and organize what they want to say. I nearly always contribute to the discussion. My goal is often for everyone to participate in some way at some point in the classroom. Broadening my understandings of how silence is a substantial contribution to the classroom community has allowed me to extend this idea to ensure that everyone participates in each class through modes other than talk.

I noticed one year that a couple of student teachers dominated most of the talk in my elementary literacy methods class. Invariably, when I posed a question, the same six people raised their hands to respond. At the same time, there were about six student teachers who were generally silent and rarely contributed to whole-group conversations. Although I was not worried about their silence per se, I wanted to make sure that they were actively engaged in the content of the class. It worried me that the student teachers of color were noticeably quieter than the White students. I considered talking to the whole class; however, initially I decided to speak individually with both the more talkative and the quieter student teachers. I asked the talkative student teachers to pause before they spoke in order to leave space for their peers. When I asked the quieter student teachers about how they saw themselves in terms of their participation in the class, they responded in a variety of ways. One explained that she was used to a different dynamic in her college classes and that she had decided to participate only in small groups. Others said that they would work to increase their verbal participation. I gave them a variety of alternatives, encouraging them to find a way to check in with me periodically through talk or writing. Within weeks, I noticed more engagement through talk, writing, and silence. Once we had established a greater level of comfort, I found ways to weave discussions about participation and silence into our whole-class conversations about teaching, providing openings for student teachers to reflect on their roles in the classroom discussions and the roles played by their peers. I modeled this discussion by articulating my teaching decisions aloud, encouraging them to speak about their roles and decisions as learners in the class. We also connected this discussion to their observation of talk and silence in their elementary school classrooms.

A teacher might also look at the topics he incorporates into his classroom. Although some topics, such as race and racism, might engender silence, they may be important to address, and there are many ways to address these topics that lessen participants' fear. Other topics might be too abstract or remote to draw students into a discussion. On the other hand, teachers might consider how they frame issues and conversations. For instance, Gallas (1995) built her elementary science curriculum around students' intrinsic curiosity and questions. At first, she used the exact wording given by the students, proposing the following kinds of questions to structure classroom discussions: What is gravity? How do plants grow? Why do leaves change color? Where do dreams come from? (Gallas, 1995, 1998, in Rymes, 2008). She found that, invariably, when she used the students' own language, a small group of students with impressive science vocabularies dominated the discussions. Through an analysis of the discourse in her classroom, including who talked and who remained silent, Gallas learned that when she revised the students' questions to make them connect more closely to children's lives, more students joined the conversation. For instance, she reframed the question "What is gravity?" posed by one student to "What happens when you jump up and down?", and she changed the student's question "Where do dreams come from?" to "Where do *your* dreams come from?" As Gallas (1995) explains, after 5 years of watching Science Talks, structured conversations about scientific topics, "I was able to see from the development of this class as talkers that even the phrasing of a question, whether asked by an adult or a child, can silence (and thereby exclude) some children" (p. 95). A teacher might look closely at her own patterns of asking questions to ascertain whether and how she has invited students to participate verbally in discussions. As Gallas demonstrates, it is not sufficient simply to use the students' own words to prompt conversations; it is crucial to think carefully about what questions and topics open up talk to a wide group of students.

Teachers can also pay attention to turn-taking norms in the classroom, negotiating these with students so that they are conscious of how often they do and do not participate in various discussions. In their study of

Alaskan natives, Scollon and Scollon (1981) report that the Athabaskan Indians took more time than their White peers to respond to teacher questions, and their pauses were just long enough for their English-speaking classmates to jump in. (See also Erickson, 1996; Rymes, 2008.) Student silence may be a product of timing. Teachers can structure conversations, allowing students to predict when it is their turn to speak. To increase verbal participation for older students, teachers might ask students to write briefly before talking aloud. With students of all ages and, in particular, younger students, teachers can ask students to turn and talk with a partner before a whole-group discussion. Some teachers of young children ask the students to sit in assigned pairs when they listen to stories so that they have a predictable partner (sometimes called a "shoulder partner") for these discussions. These same partners can be used during more formal instructional times such as Guided Reading Groups, small groups of readers focused on learning specific reading strategies. Writing and talking informally may give students the courage they need to speak aloud in class and provide everyone with practice and time to gather thoughts.

Amelia Coleman, the teacher featured in Chapter 4, encouraged students to read stories aloud for one another, which allowed more people to add their ideas verbally to the public domain without actually speaking in front of the class themselves. As I have emphasized throughout the book, shifting time frames and adding multiple modalities allows more people to participate in classroom life. Redefining participation to include silence widens the net further as teachers notice a broader range of practices that count as classroom participation.

One way to focus on forms of participation other than standard verbal contributions is to notice what is *not* said and who is *not* speaking alongside the content of a classroom conversation. This calls for shifting figure and ground, making speech that is absent as salient as that which is spoken aloud. Teachers can do this by informally keeping track of which topics are talked about and which are omitted as well as who actively (and verbally) participates in the discussion, who participates through silence, and who does not appear to participate at all. This can be done through making notations on index cards or in a small journal that a teacher keeps available for this purpose. Or, a teacher might audio- or videotape a conversation and review it with colleagues in order to do this analysis. It is difficult for a teacher to learn to see or recognize contributions that are not verbal, and this takes practice. In her book *Trusting What You Know*, Miriam Raider-Roth (2005) offers a helpful listening guide that suggests how teachers might listen both to what their students say and to their silences.

During one discussion, the teacher might pay attention to the students who rarely speak and notice how their bodies are positioned relative to the group, whether or not they are nodding, and where their eyes are directed. A teacher might focus on facial expressions, noticing whether or not and how a student is tracking the conversation. Making these judgments is tricky because some people pay attention by looking at the ceiling, while others pay attention when they look directly at the teacher. This may be an instance when it is not only desirable but necessary to include students in an investigation, asking them to describe *how* they participate in discussions or asking them to join the teacher in noticing patterns of participation in the classroom. Rather than directly confronting students about their lack of participation, teachers may want to begin with observations and descriptions. For instance, a teacher might say, "When I am reading I notice that you . . .". Following this observation, a teacher might ask the student to comment on her own activity. Asking a peer or student teacher to act as an outside observer in the classroom (or asking students to take turns tracking this information) is another way to collect data on the conditions for talk and silence in a classroom. Engaging in classroom observation and discussion with colleagues enables teachers to see their classrooms from new perspectives.

It is critical that teachers are careful not to let students get away with silence in order to opt out of engagement in classroom activity. Leaving room for silence is a potentially dangerous path to follow; such a practice might even be interpreted as a way to limit participation by individuals or groups of students. For instance, a teacher might find it easier to allow a particularly contentious student or group of students to remain silent instead of engaging with their critical contributions. In addition, if a teacher sees her responsibility, in part, as preparing students for their future education, it may be necessary to teach students to participate in recognizable ways in the future while also acknowledging the types of participation that are allowed in a particular classroom. Rather than advocating silence, I suggest that teachers inquire into the meanings of silence with students and attempt to understand what it indicates about students' responses to ongoing classroom interactions. I urge teachers to listen deeply to both talk and silence. Above all, inquiring into silence might lead to classrooms where engaged and equitable participation is defined as broadly as possible.

INVESTIGATING SILENCE WHILE LEARNING TO TEACH

Teacher education classrooms are often viewed as laboratories to model teaching methods. As a result, teacher educators often teach using methods that they would like their students—the prospective teachers—to adapt to their preschool through 12th-grade settings. I usually conclude each of my elementary literacy methods classes with a reflection on the pedagogical practices that I used during that class. I invite students to talk about how well they worked, and how (and whether) they might be adapted to the prospective teachers' grade school classrooms. At times, these discussions lead to interrogations into the role of talk and silence in our teacher education classroom. As we reflect back on the class, we address classroom dynamics and the forms of participation. For instance, I ask the prospective teachers to reflect on all of the ways that they participated during the class session. We can explore whether these are verbal and/or nonverbal modes of participation. This might lead to inquiries similar to the ones I have described in their elementary classrooms. Practicing this inquiry stance in a teacher education classroom opens up the conversation about how to adapt the practice in K–12 settings. For instance, I might explore, with the prospective teachers, the conditions that support talk and silence in our teacher education classroom. Further, we might investigate the conditions that support various forms of participation in the course. Explicit talk about how to modify these investigations for K–12 classrooms is central to the work of teacher education.

In order to generate discussions about the relationships among silence, talk, and participation, I ask prospective teachers to informally document the silences in their K–12 classrooms and to bring those notes and reflections to our class. Most prospective teachers document the silence of individuals. Some notice the ways that the class is silent during certain times of the day. They attribute the silence to individuals and, less frequently, to the teacher. Often, they document more episodic examples of silence— silence around certain topics, silence by students in response to comments made by teachers, or silence that, on the surface, seems inexplicable— rather than broader patterns that can only be discerned over time. We look across the data collected during the week for themes to generate a discussion about classroom silence. This simple exercise allows prospective teachers to become more aware of how silence works in their classrooms, and afterward, they are invariably more attuned to it and bring it into our discussions with greater frequency.

RETHINKING PARTICIPATION

In his poem, "Thirteen Ways of Looking at a Blackbird," Wallace Stevens (1923) writes:

I do not know which to prefer,
The beauty of inflections
Or the beauty of innuendoes,
The blackbird whistling
Or just after.

In teaching, as in most interactions, we tend to focus on the blackbird's song rather than the time and the space that comes just after. What would it mean as educators to learn to understand the meanings conveyed by both silence and talk as essential components of classroom participation? In this book, I define participation as contribution and connection. I link this understanding to conceptions of democratic participation, suggesting that broadening our understanding of how students participate in classrooms leads to more inclusive and equitable education that draws on multiple viewpoints and experiences. Taking a sociocultural perspective, I unpack the various functions and uses of silence by teachers and students in order to understand how participation might include silence, the space that comes after or surrounds talk. I suggest that teachers might shift participation structures, include a variety of modalities, and learn to read nonverbal as well as verbal contributions. The term *participatory presence*, introduced in Chapter 4, captures how students might be engaged in the classroom community without using more typical verbal strategies. Finally, I urge teachers and students to join together to inquire into silence and talk in their classrooms.

In nearly every classroom—kindergarten or college; urban, suburban, or rural; in the United States or Aceh, Indonesia—there are students who are silent. My hope is that this book helps educators, and possibly students themselves, hold larger understandings of these silences, locating the silences in the social context as much as the individual, and finding ways to make silence an affirmative part of the classroom dynamic, rather than simply a negation. As educators, we must work toward recognizing, including, and understanding the diverse modes of participation that students bring to classrooms. This is not to say that all contributions are useful and move learning forward, but rather that broader conceptions of participation that encompass a wide range of ways to join classroom activity and conversation allow for greater access, deeper understanding of diverse perspectives, and the generation of new knowledge. Reconceptualizing participation in this manner allows educators to truly hear silent voices.

Partial Transcript of the Author's Chair Event

Note: The numbers in parentheses indicate the seconds of silence. The description in brackets indicates the nonverbal activities. The brackets align the silence and nonverbal activities with the talk. Additional transcript conventions include the following: A colon (:) indicates an elongated syllable or sound. The speech is in **bold** and nonverbal interactions are in *italics*. Transcription prepared by Kathryn Howard. (See also Howard, 2006; Schultz, 2006a.)

M Davis   **let's hea:r [f:ro:m=**
Terrell   *[(raises hand, looking at teacher,*
M Davis   **=[(1.4)**
M Davis   *[(looks away from Terrell, [looks back toward Terrell)*
Terrell   *[(raises hand again, looking at teacher)*
M Davis   **[from Terre:ll?**
M Davis   *[(touches Terrell on the back, looking at him)*
Terrell   (Stands up with booklet, walks to chair, sits down, orients the
    booklet, opens to first page)
Girl(?)   **we're all excited [Terrell**
M Davis   **[and his titl- your facts is abou:t,**
    [(3.0)
Terrell   *[(flips back to front cover of booklet, looks at it)*
Boy(?)   *((quietly))* **being a better writer.**
Terrell   **being a better writer.**
    [(10.0)
Terrell   *[(opens booklet to first page, flashes his eyes over to right, carefully*
    folds back front cover, flashes his eyes to the left, keeps folding, then flashes
    his eyes to right again, looks down at page)
Terrell   **I:, (5.0) want (0.2) to: (0.2) be: ay (1.0)**
    [better: [(0.4)   [writer
Terrell   *[(looks at teacher, [looks at page, [looks at teacher)*
    (1.5)
Terrell   **I:, (1.5) want (0.2) to:**
    [(5.0)

Terrell   [*(looking intently at the page)*
Taisha   **((quietly))[()**
Terrell   [*(looks at Taisha*
Dillon   **((quietly)) [(I know/mmm) (I'm trying to) help him**
Terrell   [*(looks at Dillon as he approaches*
Dillon   [*(walks on knees up to Terrell's chair, grabs paper (Terrell still holds it), turns it toward himself and looks at the page)*
Dillon   *((quietly))* **ruh- (0.2) [writer,**
Dillon   [*(looking at Terrell)*
Terrell   **writer:,**
        [(5.0)
        [*(Terrell pulls booklet out of Dillon's hands, looks down at page)*
        [[(10.0)
Terrell   [[*glances at several students in front and to the right, and back to his page. Shawn (on right) walks on knees up to his chair, Terrell points to a particular spot on the page, Shawn looks at page)*
Shawn   [*((whispers something—inaudible))*
Shawn   [*(looking up at Terrell, sits back down as he whispers again)*
Terrell   **neatly:,**
        [(24.0)
Terrell   [*(Terrell opens his page and shows it to a student on the right, nods, then carefully turns the page and folds open his booklet to that page. Looks at page for several seconds, then looks at Taisha.)*
Taisha   [*(comes next to Terrell on her knees, looks at page as Terrell points at a word)*
Taisha   *((whispering))* **[with**
Taisha   [*(looking at Terrell, stays kneeling next to him)*
Terrell   **[with, (0.2) my: (0.2) mo:m: () (Terrell Cole,)**
Terrell   [*(looking intently at page as he reads*
Taisha   [*(looking from page to Terrell as he reads)*
        (0.6)
Terrell   [*(looking intently at page with finger pointing at a word)*
Terrell   **my: (0.2) mom (1.0) a:nd (0.2) da:d,**
        [(12.0)
Terrell   [*(looks over to right, then looks at page pointing to it, glances at Dillon, then back at page, glances at Shawn on right, folds page and points at word as Shawn walks on knees up to Terrell's chair)*
Terrell   **want,**
Dillon   [[[*(walks on knees next to Terrell, pulls on Terrell's hand toward him to look at the page)*
        (2.0)
?   *((quietly))* **to**

      (6.0)
Terrell   **be:**
      (3.0)
Taisha? **ay,**
      (3.0)
Taisha   *[(stands up behind Terrell)*
Terrell   **better writer:**
      (5.0)
?   [(   )
Shawn & Dillon   *[(looking at Terrell)*
Terrell   **(letter/better,?) (0.5) from:. (0.2) fro:m? (0.4) Terrell Cole.**
M Davis **let's give him a thumb's up.**
Terrell   **Thank you.**
Taisha   *(gives a thumb's up next to Terrell's face)*
M Davis **(alright/people) remember these are works in pro:gress.**
    (0.8) a big thumb's up.

References

Alvermann, D. E., O'Brien, D. G., & Dillon, D. R. (1990). What teachers do when they say they're having discussions of content area reading assignments: A qualitative analysis. *Reading Research Quarterly, 25*(4), 296–322.

Anderson, G. L. (1998). Toward authentic participation: Deconstructing the discourses of participatory reforms in education. *American Educational Research Journal, 35*(4), 571–603.

Apple, M. (1979). *Ideology and curriculum.* New York: Routledge.

Apple, M. (2000). *Official knowledge: Democratic education in a conservative age* (2nd ed.). New York: Routledge.

Au, K. H., & Jordan, C. (1981). Teaching reading to Hawaiian children: Finding a culturally appropriate solution. In H. T. Trueba, G. P. Guthrie, & K. H. Au (Eds.), *Culture in the bilingual classroom: Studies in classroom ethnography* (pp. 139–152). Rowley, MA: Newberry House.

Au, K. H., & Mason, J. M. (1981). Social organizational factors in learning to read: The balance of rights hypothesis. *Reading Research Quarterly, 17*(1), 115–152.

Bakhtin, M. (1981). *The dialogic imagination* (C. Emerson & M. Holquist, Trans.). Austin: The University of Texas Press.

Ball, D. L. (1997). What do students know?: Facing challenges of distance, context, and desire in trying to hear children. In B. J. Biddle, T. L. Good, & I. F. Goodson (Eds.), *International handbook of teachers and teaching* (pp. 769–818). Boston: Kluwer Academic Publishers.

Ball, D. L. (1993). With an eye on the mathematical horizon: Dilemmas of teaching elementary school mathematics. *Elementary School Journal, 93*(4), 373–397.

Ball, D. L., & Cohen, D. K. (1999). Developing practice, developing practitioners: Toward a practice-based theory of professional education. In L. Darling-Hammond & G. Sykes (Eds.), *Teaching as the learning profession: Handbook of policy and research* (pp. 3–32). San Francisco: Jossey-Bass.

Banks, J. A. (1993a). The canon debate, knowledge construction, and multicultural education. *Educational Researcher, 22*(5), 4–14.

Banks, J. A. (1993b). Multicultural education: Historical development, dimensions, and practice. *Review of Research in Education, 19*, 3–49.

Baquedano-Lopez, P. (2004). Literacy practices across learning contexts. In A. Duranti (Ed.), *A companion to linguistic anthropology* (pp. 245–268). Malden, MA: Blackwell.

Basso, K. H. (1979). *Portraits of "The Whiteman": Linguistic play and cultural symbols among the western Apache*. New York: Cambridge University Press.

Basso, K. H. (1990). *Western Apache language and culture: Essays in linguistic anthropology*. Tucson: University of Arizona Press.

Basso, K. H. (1996). *Wisdom sits in places: Landscape and language among the Western Apache*. Albuquerque: University of New Mexico Press.

Baumann, R. (1983). *Let your words be few: Symbolism of speaking and silence among seventeenth-century Quakers*. Cambridge: Cambridge University Press.

Bean, J. C., & Peterson, D. Grading class participation. (n.d.). Retrieved April 9, 2008, from www.csufresno.edu/academics/documents/grading_class_participation

Blackburn, M. V. (2002/2003). Disrupting the (hetero)normative: Exploring literacy performances and identity work with queer youth. *Journal of Adolescent and Adult Literacy, 46*(4), 312–324.

Boal, A. (2002). *Games for actors and non-actors* (A. Jackson, Trans.). New York: Routledge.

Boal, A. (2000). *Theater of the oppressed* (C. A. & M. L. McBride & E. Fryer, Trans.). London: Pluto.

Boaler, J., & Humphreys, C. (2005). *Connecting mathematical ideas: Middle school video cases to support teaching & learning*. Portsmouth, NH: Heinemann.

Bock, P. K. (1976). "I think but dare not speak": Silence in Elizabethan culture. *Journal of Anthropological Research, 32*, 285–294.

Bosacki, S. L. (2005). *The culture of classroom silence*. New York: Peter Lang.

Braithwaite, C. A. (1985). Cultural uses and interpretations of silence. In D. Tannen & M. Saville-Troike (Eds.), *Perspectives on silence* (pp. 163–172). Norwood, NJ: Ablex.

Brayboy, B. M. (2004). Hiding in the Ivy: American Indian students and visibility in elite educational settings. *Harvard Educational Review, 74*(2), 125–152.

Brown, L. M., & Gilligan, C. (1992). *Meeting at the crossroads: Women's psychology and girls' development*. Cambridge, MA: Harvard University Press.

Buck, P., & Skilton-Sylvester, P. (2005). Preservice teachers enter urban communities: Coupling funds of knowledge research and critical pedagogy in teacher education. In N. González, L. C. Moll, & C. Amanti (Eds.), *Funds of knowledge: Theorizing practices in households, communities, and classrooms* (pp. 213–232). Mahwah, NJ: Lawrence Erlbaum Associates.

Burbules, N. (2004). Introduction. In M. Boler (Ed.), *Democratic dialogue in education: Troubling speech, disturbing silence* (pp. xiii–xxxii). New York: Peter Lang.

Cage, J. M. (1961). *Silence: Letters and writing*. Middletown, CT: Wesleyan University Press.

Cage, J. M. (1973). *Writings '67–72*. Middletown, CT: Wesleyan University Press.

Cammarota, J., & Fine, M. (2008). *Revolutionizing education: Youth participatory action research in motion*. New York: Routledge.

Campano, G. (2007). *Immigrant students and literacy: Reading, writing, and remembering*. New York: Teachers College Press.

Carter, S. P. (2001). *The possibilities of silence: African-American female cultural identity and secondary English classrooms*. Unpublished doctoral dissertation, Vanderbilt University, Nashville.

Cazden, C. B. (2001). *Classroom discourse: The language of teaching and learning* (2nd ed.). Portsmouth, NH: Heinemann.

Cha, T. H. K. (1995). *Dictee*. Berkeley, CA: Third Woman Press.

Cheung, K. (1993). *Articulate silences: Kisaye Yamamoto, Maxine Hong Kingston, Joy Kogawa*. Ithaca, NY: Cornell University Press.

Christensen, L. (2000). *Reading, writing, and rising up: Teaching about social justice and the power of the written word*. Milwaukee, WI: Rethinking Schools.

Clair, R. P. (1998). *Organizing silence: A world of possibilities*. Albany, NY: SUNY Press.

Cochran-Smith, M., & Lytle, S. L. (1999). Relationships of knowledge and practice: Teacher learning in communities. In A. Iran-Nejad & C. D. Pearson (Eds.), *Review of research in education* (pp. 249–306). Washington, DC: American Educational Research Association.

Constable, M. (2005). *Just silences: The limits and possibilities of modern law*. Princeton, NJ: Princeton University Press.

Cook-Sather, A. (2002). Authorizing students' perspectives: Towards trust, dialogue, and change in education. *Educational Researcher, 31*(4), 3–14.

Cook-Sather, A. (2006). Sound, presence, and power: Exploring "student voice" in educational research and reform. *Curriculum Inquiry, 36*(4), 359–390.

Darling-Hammond, L. (1996). The right to learn and the advancement of teaching: Research, policy, and practice for democratic education. *Educational Researcher, 25*(6), 5–17.

Delpit, L. (1995). *Other people's children: Cultural conflict in the classroom*. New York: The New Press.

Dewey, J. (1944). *Democracy and education*. New York: The Free Press (Original work published in 1916)

Dumont, R. V. (1972). Learning English and how to be silent: Studies in Sioux and Cherokee classrooms. In C. Cazden, V. P. Johns, & D. Hymes (Eds.), *Functions of language in the classroom* (pp. 344–369). Prospect Heights, IL: Waveland Press.

Duncan, P. (2004). *Tell this silence: Asian American women writers and the politics of speech*. Iowa City: University of Iowa Press.

Dyson, A. H. (2003). "Welcome to the Jam": Popular culture, school literacy, and the making of childhoods. *Harvard Educational Review, 73*(3), 328–361.

Erickson, F. (1996). Going for the zone: The social and cognitive ecology of teacher-student interaction in classroom conversations. In D. Hicks (Ed.), *Discourse, learning, and schooling* (pp. 29–62). Cambridge: Cambridge University Press.

Erickson, F., & Mohatt, G. (1982). Cultural organization of participation structures in two classrooms of Indian students. In G. Spindler (Ed.), *Doing the ethnography of schooling* (pp. 132–174). New York: Holt, Rinehart and Winston.

Finders, M. J. (1996). Queens and teen zines: Early adolescent females reading their way toward adulthood. *Anthropology and Education Quarterly 27*(1), 71–89.

Fine, M. (1987). Silencing in public school. *Language Arts, 64*(2), 157–174.

Fine, M. (1991). *Framing dropouts: Notes on the politics of an urban high school*. Albany: State University of New York Press.

Fine, M., Roberts, R. A., & Torre, M. E. (2004). *Echoes of Brown: Youth documenting and performing the legacy of Brown v. Board of Education.* New York: Teachers College Press.

Fine, M., Torre, M. E., Burns, A., & Payne, Y. A. (2007). Youth research/participatory methods for reform. In D. Thiessen and A. Cook-Sather (Eds.), *International handbook of student experience in elementary and secondary school* (pp. 805–828). New York: Springer.

Foley, D. E. (1995). *The heartland chronicles.* Philadelphia: University of Pennsylvania Press.

Foley, D. E. (1996). The silent Indian as a cultural production. In B. Levinson, D. Foley, & D. Holland (Eds.), *The cultural production of a person: Critical ethnographies of school and local practice* (pp. 79–92). Albany: State University of New York Press.

Fordham, S. (1993). Those loud Black girls: (Black) women, silence, and gender "passing" in the Academy. *Anthropology and Education Quarterly, 24*(1), 3–32.

Fordham, S. (1996). *Blacked out: Dilemmas of race, identity, and success at Capital High.* Chicago: University of Chicago Press.

Foucault, M. (1977). *Discipline and punish: The birth of the prison* (A. M. Sheridan-Smith, Trans.). Harmondsworth, UK: Penguin.

Fountas, I. C., & Pinnell, G. S. (1996). *Guided reading: Good first teaching for all children.* Portsmouth, NH: Heinemann.

Freire, P. (1970). *Pedagogy of the oppressed.* New York: Herder and Herder.

Gal, S. (1991). Between speech and silence. In M. di Leonardo (Ed.), *Gender at the crossroads of knowledge: Feminist anthropology in the postmodern era* (pp. 175–203). Berkeley: University of California Press.

Gallas, K. (1995). *Talking their way into science: Hearing children's questions and theories, responding with curriculum.* New York: Teachers College Press.

Gallas, K. (1998). *"Sometimes I can be anything": Power, gender, and identity in a primary classroom.* New York: Teachers College Press.

Gay, G. (2000). *Cultural responsive teaching: Theory, research, and practice.* New York: Teachers College Press.

Gee, J. P. (1996). *Social linguistics and literacies: Ideology in discourses* (2nd ed.). London: The Falmer Press.

Gee, J. P. (2003). *What video games have to teach us about learning and literacy.* New York: Palgrave Macmillan.

Gilligan, C. (1982). *In a different voice: Psychological theory and women's development.* Cambridge, MA: Harvard University Press.

Gilmore, P. (1983). Spelling "Mississippi:" Recontextualizing a literacy event. *Anthropology and Education Quarterly, 14*(4), 235–256.

Gilmore, P. (1985). Silence and sulking: Emotional displays in the classroom. In D. Tannen & M. Saville-Troike (Eds.), *Perspectives on silence* (pp. 139–162). Norwood, NJ: Ablex.

Goffman, E. (1974). *Frame analysis: An essay on the organization of experience.* Cambridge, MA: Harvard University Press.

Goffman, E. (1981). *Forms of talk.* Philadelphia: University of Pennsylvania Press.

Goldberger, N. R., Tarule, J. M., Clinchy, B. M., & Belenky, M. F. (Eds.). (1996).

Knowledge, difference, and power: Essays inspired by women's ways of knowing. New York: Basic Books.

González, N., Moll, L. C., & Amanti, C. (Eds.). (2005). *Funds of knowledge: Theorizing practices in households, communities, and classrooms.* Mahwah, NJ: Lawrence Erlbaum Associates.

Goodlad, J. L. (1984). *A place called school: Prospects for the future.* New York: McGraw-Hill.

Goodwin, M. H. (1990). *He-said-she-said: Talk as social organization among Black children.* Bloomington: Indiana University Press.

Goodwin, M. H. (2001). Participation. In A. Duranti (Ed.), *Key terms in language and culture* (pp. 172–175). Malden, MA: Blackwell Publishing.

Goodwin, C., & Goodwin, M. H. (2004). Participation. In A. Duranti (Ed.), *A companion to linguistic anthropology* (pp. 222–244). Malden, MA: Blackwell Publishing.

Granger, C. A. (2004). *Silence in second language learning: A psychoanalytic reading.* Clevedon, UK: Multilingual Matters.

Greene, M. (1988). *The dialectic of freedom.* New York: Teachers College Press.

Greene, M. (1995). *Releasing the imagination: Essays on education, the arts, and social change.* San Francisco, CA: Jossey-Bass.

Greene, M. (2003). Teaching as possibility: A light in dark times. In *The Jossey-Bass reader on teaching.* San Francisco: John Wiley.

Greeno, J. G. (1997). On claims that answer the wrong questions, *Educational Researcher, 26*(1), 5–17.

Heath, S. B. (1982). Protean shapes in literacy events: Ever-shifting oral and literate traditions. In D. Tannen (Ed.), *Spoken and written language: Exploring orality and literacy* (pp. 91–118). Norwood, NJ: Ablex.

Heath, S. B. (1998). Living the arts through language plus learning: A report on community-based youth organizations. *Americans for the Arts Monographs, 2*(7), 1–19.

Heath, S. B. (2000). Seeing our way into learning. *Cambridge Journal of Education, 30*(1), 121–132.

Hiebert, J., Carpenter, T. P., Fennema, E., Fuson, K., Wearne, D., Murray, H., Olivier, A., & Human, P. (1997). *Making sense: Teaching and learning mathematics with understanding.* Portsmouth, NH: Heinemann.

Hoffman, M. (1991). *Amazing Grace.* New York: Dial Books.

Holland, D., Lachicotte, W., Skinner, D., & Cain, C. (1998). *Identity and agency in cultural worlds.* Cambridge, MA: Harvard University Press.

hooks, b. (1989) *Talking back: Thinking feminist, thinking black.* Boston: South End Press.

hooks, b. (2004). *Skin again.* New York: Jump at the Sun/Hyperion.

Hori, G. V. S. (1994). Teaching and learning in the Rinzai Zen monastery. *Journal of Japanese Studies, 20*(1), 5–35.

Howard, K. M. (2006, March). *Microethnography in language and literacy research.* Paper presented at TESOL Conference, Orlando, FL.

Hull, G. (2003). At last: Youth culture and digital media: New literacies for new times. *Research in the Teaching of English, 38,* 229–233.

Hull, G., & James, M. (2007). Geographies of hope: A study of urban landscapes and a university-community collaborative. In P. O'Neill (Ed.), *Blurring boundaries: Developing writers, researchers, and teachers: A tribute to William L. Smith* (pp. 255–289). Chicago: Hampton Press.

Hull, G., & Schultz, K. (2002). *School's out: Bridging out of school literacies with classroom practice.* New York: Teachers College Press.

Hymes, D. (1964). Introduction: Towards ethnographies of communication. In J. J. Gumperz & D. Hymes (Eds.), *The ethnography of communication* (pp. 1–34). Washington, DC: American Anthropology Association.

Hymes, D. H. (1967). Models of the interaction of language and social setting. *Journal of Social Issues, 23*(2), 8–28.

Jensen, J. V. (1973). Communicative functions of silence. *ETC: A Review of General Semantics, 30*(3), 249–257.

Kaomea, J. (2003). Reading erasures and making the familiar strange: Defamiliarizing methods for research in formerly colonized and historically oppressed communities. *Educational Researcher, 32*(2), 14–23.

Kingston, M. H. (1989). *Woman warrior: Memoirs of a girlhood among ghosts.* New York: Random House.

Kliebard, H. M. (1966). *The struggle for the American curriculum: 1893–1958.* New York: Routledge.

Kogawa, J. (1982). *Obasan.* Boston: D. R. Godine.

Kohl, H. R. (1994). *I won't learn from you: And other thoughts on creative maladjustment.* New York: New Press.

Labaree, D. F. (1997). Public goods, private goods: The American struggle over educational goals. *American Educational Research Journal, 34*(1), 39–81.

Ladson-Billings, G. (1994). *The Dreamkeepers: Successful teachers of African-American children.* San Francisco: Jossey-Bass.

Ladson-Billings, G. (1996). Silences as weapons: Challenges of a Black professor teaching White students. *Theory into Practice, 35*(2), 79–86.

Ladson-Billings, G. (2003). New directions in multicultural education: Complexities, boundaries, and critical race theory. In J. A. Banks & C. A. McGee Banks (Eds.), *Handbook of research on multicultural education* (2nd ed.) (pp. 50–68). San Francisco: Jossey-Bass.

Lave, J., & Wenger, E. (1991). *Situated learning: Legitimate peripheral participation.* New York: Cambridge University Press.

Lebra, T. S. (1987). The cultural significance of silence in Japanese communication. *Multilingua, 6*(4), 634–657.

Lee, S. J. (2005). *Up against whiteness: Race, school, and immigrant youth.* New York: Teachers College Press.

Levy, S. (1996). *Starting from scratch: One classroom builds its own curriculum.* Portsmouth, NH: Heinemann.

Lewis, M. (1993). *Without a word: Teaching beyond women's silence.* New York: Routledge.

Li, Huey L. (2004). Rethinking silencing silences. In M. Boler (Ed.), *Democratic dialogue in education: Troubling speech, disturbing silence* (pp. 69–86). New York: Peter Lang.

Lorde, A. (1984). *Sister outsider: Essays and speeches.* Trumansburg, NY: Crossing Press.

Lorde, A. (1997). *The collected poems of Audre Lorde.* New York: W. W. Norton.

Lomawaima, T., & McCarty, T. L. (2006). *"To remain an Indian": Lessons in democracy from a century of Native American education.* New York: Teachers College Press.

MacKendrick, K. (2001). *Immemorial silence.* Albany: SUNY Press.

Maclear, K. (1994). Not in so many words: Translating silence across "difference." *Fireweed: A Feminist Quarterly of Writing, Politics, Art and Culture, 44–45,* 6–11.

McCarthy, C. (1988). Reconsidering liberal and radical perspectives on racial inequality in schooling: Making the case for nonsynchrony. *Harvard Educational Review, 58,* 265–279.

McCarthy, C. (1993). Multicultural approaches to racial inequality in the United States. In L. A. Castenell, Jr. and W. F. Pinar (Eds.), *Understanding curriculum as racial text: Representations of identity and difference in education* (pp. 225–246). Albany: SUNY Press.

McCarty, T. l., Lynch, R. H., Wallace, S., & Benally, A. (1991). Classroom inquiry and native learning styles: A call for reassessment. *Anthropology and Education Quarterly, 22*(1), 42–59.

McDermott, R. P. (1974). Achieving school failure: An anthropological approach to illiteracy and social stratification. In G. Spindler (Ed.), *Education and cultural process: Toward an anthropology of education* (pp. 82–118). New York: Holt, Rinehart and Winston.

McDermott, R. P. (1987). The explanation of minority school failure, again. *Anthropology & Education Quarterly, 18*(4), 361–367.

McDermott, R. P. (1988). Inarticulateness. In D. Tannen (Ed.), *Linguistics in context* (pp. 34–68). Norwood, NJ: Ablex.

McDermott, R. P., & Gospodinoff, K. (1979). Social contexts for ethnic borders and school failure. In A. Wolfgang (Ed.), *Nonverbal behavior: Applications and cultural implications* (pp. 175–195). New York: Academic Press.

McIntyre, A. (2000). *Inner-city kids: Adolescents confront life and violence in an urban community.* New York: New York University Press.

Mehan, H. (1979). *Learning lessons.* Cambridge, MA: Harvard University Press.

Minh-ha, T. T. (1990). Not you/like you: Post-colonial women and the interlocking questions of identity and difference. In G. Anzaldúa (Ed.), *Making face, making soul/Haciendo caras: Creative and critical perspectives by women of color* (pp. 371–375). San Francisco: Aunt Lute Books.

Moll, L. C. (1992). Bilingual classroom studies and community analysis: Some recent trends. *Educational Researcher, 21*(3), 20–24.

Moll, L. C., & Greenberg, J. B. (1990). Creating zones of possibilities: Combining social context for instruction. In L. C. Moll (Ed.), *Vygotsky and education: Instructional implications and applications of sociohistorical psychology* (pp. 319–348). Cambridge, UK: Cambridge University Press.

Momaday, N. S. (1997). *The man made of words: Essays, stories, passages.* New York: St. Martin's Press.

Nieto, S. (2000). *Affirming diversity: The sociopolitical context of multicultural education* (3rd ed.). New York: Longman.

Nwoye, G. (1985). Eloquent silence among the Igbo of Nigeria. In D. Tannen & M. Saville-Troike (Eds.), *Perspectives on silence* (pp. 185–191). Norwood, NJ: Ablex.

Ortega y Gassett, J. (1957). *Man and people* (W. R. Trask, Trans.). New York: Norton.

Philips, S. U. (1972). Participant structures and communicative competence: Warm Springs Indians in community and classroom. In C. B. Cazden, V. P. John, & D. Hymes (Eds.), *Functions of language in the classroom* (pp. 370–394). Prospect Heights, IL: Waveland Press.

Philips, S. U. (1983). *The invisible culture: Communication in classroom and community on the Warm Springs Indian Reservation.* New York: Longman.

Picard, M. (1948/1952). *The world of silence* (S. Goldman, Trans.). Chicago: Henry Regnery.

Pollock, M. (2004). *Colormute: Race dilemmas in an American school.* Princeton, NJ: Princeton University Press.

Pollock, M. (2008). *Everyday antiracism: Concrete ways to successfully navigate the relevance of race in school.* New York: The New Press.

Raider-Roth, M. B. (2005). *Trusting what you know: The high stakes of classroom relationships.* San Francisco: Jossey-Bass.

Remillard, J. T., & Geist, P. K. (2002). Supporting teachers' professional learning by navigating openings in the curriculum. *Journal of Mathematics Teacher Education, 5*(1), 1386–4416.

Rich, A. (1979). *On lies, secrets, and silence: Selected prose, 1966–1978.* New York: W. W. Norton.

Rich, A. (1984). *The fact of a doorframe: Poems selected and new 1950–1984.* New York: W. W. Norton.

Rodgers, C. R., & Raider-Roth, M. B. (2006). Presence in teaching. *Teachers and Teaching, 12*(3), 265–287.

Rogers, A. G. (1993). Voice, play, and a practice of ordinary courage in girls' and women's lives. *Harvard Educational Review, 63*(3), 265–295.

Rogers, A. G. (2006). *The unsayable: The hidden language of trauma.* New York: Random House.

Roosevelt, D. (1998a). "There the kid was, stranded in the car": Reading the fictions of children as if they mattered. *Curriculum Inquiry, 28*(1), 81–111.

Roosevelt, D. (1998b). Unsuspected literatures: Public school classrooms as laboratories for the creation of democratic culture. *Theory into Practice, 37*(4), 271–279.

Rowe, M. B. (1986). Wait time: Slowing down may be a way of speeding up. *Journal of Teacher Education, 37*(1), 736–741.

Rymes, B. R. (2008). *Classroom discourse analysis: A tool for critical reflection.* Cresskill, NJ: Hampton Press.

Rymes, B. R., Cahnmann-Taylor, M., & Souto-Manning, M. (2008). Bilingual teachers' performances of power and conflict. *Teaching Education, 19*(2), 105–119.

Saville-Troike, M. (1982). *The ethnography of communication: An introduction.* Baltimore: University Park Press.

Saville-Troike, M. (1985). The place of silence in an integrated theory of communication. In D. Tannen & M. Saville-Troike (Eds.), *Perspectives on silence* (pp. 3–18). Norwood, NJ: Ablex.

Schultz, K. (2002). Looking across space and time: Reconceptualizing literacy learning in and out of school. *Research in the Teaching of English, 36*(3), 356–390.

Schultz, K. (2003). *Listening: A framework for teaching across difference.* New York: Teachers College Press.

Schultz, K. (2006a, March). *Listening to silence and participation in a first grade classroom: Towards implications for research and teaching second language learners.* Paper presented at the TESOL Conference, Tampa Bay, FL.

Schultz, K. (2006b). Qualitative research on writing. In C. A. MacArthur, S. Graham, & J. Fitzgerald (Eds.), *Handbook of writing research* (pp. 357–373). New York: Guilford Press.

Schultz, K. (2008). Interrogating students' silences. In Mica Pollock (Ed.), *Everyday antiracism: Concrete ways to successfully navigate the relevance of race in school* (pp. 217–221), New York: The New Press.

Schultz, K., Buck, P., & Niesz, T. (2000). Democratizing conversations: Discourses of "race" in a post-desegregated middle school. *American Education Research Journal, 37*(1), 33–65.

Schultz, K., Buck, P., & Niesz, T. (2005). Authoring "race": Writing truth and fiction after school. *Urban Review, 37*(5), 469–489.

Schultz, K., & Coleman, C. (2009, February). *Becoming visible in the classroom: Storytelling across multiple modalities.* Presented at meeting of the Ethnography in Education Forum, Philadelphia, PA.

Schultz, K., & Davis, J. (1996). *After desegregation: Students and teachers talk about "race" and relations in post-desegregated schools.* Proposal submitted to the Spencer Foundation, Chicago, IL.

Schultz, K., & Fecho, B. (2005). Literacies in adolescence: An analysis of policies from the United States and Queensland, Australia. In N. Bascia, A. Cumming, A. Datnow, K. Leithwood, & D. Livingstone (Eds.), *International handbook of educational policy* (pp. 677–694). Dordecht, The Netherlands: Kluwer Academic Publishers.

Schultz, K., Jones-Walker, C., & Chikkatur, A. (2008). Listening to students, negotiating beliefs: Preparing teachers for urban classrooms. *Curriculum Inquiry, 38*(2), 155–187.

Schultz, K., & Throop, R. (in press). Curriculum and popular culture. In A. Luke & D. Pearson (Eds.), *Third international encyclopedia of education curriculum development.* New York: Elsevier.

Schultz, K., Vasudevan, L., Bateman, J., & Coleman, A. (2004, February). *Storytelling across multiple modalities as method.* Presented at meeting of the Ethnography in Education Forum, Philadelphia, PA.

Schultz, K., Vasudevan, L., & Throop, R. (2007). Adolescent literacy in a global society. In B. Guzzetti (Ed.), *Literacy for the new millenium: Adolescent literacy* (pp. 12–36). Portsmouth, NH: Greenwood.

Scollon, R. (1985). The machine stops: Silence in the metaphor of malfunction. In D. Tannen & M. Saville-Troike (Eds.), *Perspectives on silence* (pp. 21–30). Norwood, NJ: Ablex.

Scollon, R., & Scollon, B. K. (1981). *Narrative, literacy, and face in interethnic communication.* Norwood, NJ: Ablex.

Skilton-Sylvester, P. (1994). Elementary school curricula and urban transformation. *Harvard Educational Review, 64*(3), 309–331.

Sontag, S. (1969). *Styles of radical will.* New York: Dell.

Spender, D. (1980). *Man made language.* London: Routledge & Kegan Paul.

Stein, P. (2004). Representation, rights, and resources: Multimodal pedagogies in the language and literacy classroom. In B. Norton & K. Toohey (Eds.), *Critical pedagogies and language learning* (pp. 95–115). Cambridge, UK: Cambridge University Press.

Stein, P., & Newfield, D. (2002). Shifting the gaze in South African classrooms: New pedagogies, new publics, new democracies. *International Journal of Learning.* Retrieved May 7, 2008, from *http://www.readingonline.org/international/stein/*

Stevens, W. (1923). *Harmonium.* New York: Alfred A. Knopf.

Strieb, L. Y. (in preparation). *Inviting families.* New York: Teachers College Press.

Tannen, D., & Saville-Troike, M. (1985a). Introduction. In D. Tannen & M. Saville-Troike (Eds.), *Perspectives on silence* (pp. xi–xviii). Norwood, NJ: Ablex.

Tannen, D., & Saville-Troike, M. (Eds.). (1985b). *Perspectives on silence* (pp. xi–xviii). Norwood, NJ: Ablex.

Tateishi, C. A. (2007/2008, Winter). Taking a chance with words. *Rethinking Schools, 22*(2). Retrieved May 7, 2008, from http://www.rethinkingschools.org/archive/22_02/word222.shtml

Taylor, J. M., Gilligan, C., & Sullivan, A. M. (1995). *Between voice and silence: Women and girls, race and relationship.* Cambridge, MA: Harvard University Press.

Thomas, A. (2004). Digital literacies of cybergirl. *E-Learning, 1*(3), 358–382.

Tomlinson, C. (1999). *The differentiated classroom: Responding to the needs of all learners.* Alexandria, VA: ASCD.

Torre, M., & Fine, M. (2006). Researching and resisting: Democratic policy research by and for youth. In S. Ginwright, P. Noguera, & J. Cammarota (Eds.), *Beyond resistance! Youth activism and community change: New democratic possibilities for practice and policy for America's youth* (pp. 269–285). New York: Routledge.

Torre, M. E., & Fine, M., with Alexander, N., Billups, A. B., Blanding, Y., Genao, E., Marboe, E., Salah, T., & Urdang, K. (2008). Participatory action research in the contact zone. In J. Cammarota & M. Fine, M. (Eds.), *Revolutionizing education: Youth participatory action research in motion* (pp. 23–44). New York: Routledge.

Van Manen, M. (1990). *Researching lived experience: Human science for an action sensitive pedagogy.* Albany: SUNY Press.

Varenne, H., & McDermott, R. P. (1999). *Successful failure: The school America builds.* Boulder, CO: Westview Press.

Vasudevan, L. (2004). *Telling different stories differently: The possibilities of multimodal (counter)storytelling with African American adolescent boys.* Unpublished dissertation. University of Pennsylvania.

Vasudevan, L., Schultz, K., & Bateman, J. (under review). Beyond the printed page: Multimodal storytelling in an urban classroom.

Vygotsky, L. S. (1978). *Mind in society: The development of higher psychological processes*. Cambridge, MA: Harvard University Press.

Walkerdine, V. (1990). *Schoolgirl fictions*. London: Verso.

Walkerdine, V., Lucey, H., & Melody, J. (2001). *Growing up girl: Psychosocial explorations of gender and class*. New York: New York University Press.

Wittengenstein, L. (1961). *Tractatus logico-philosophicus*. New York: Humanities Press.

Wortham, S. (2006). *Learning identity: The joint emergence of social identification and academic learning*. New York: Cambridge University Press.

Yamamoto, H. (1994). *Seventeen syllables* (K-K Cheung, Ed.). New Brunswick, NJ: Rutgers University Press.

Zembylas, M., & Michaelides, P. (2004). The sound of silence in pedagogy. *Educational Theory, 54*(2), 193–210.

Index

About the Author

KATHERINE SCHULTZ is an associate professor of education at the University of Pennsylvania and the director of the Center for Collaborative Research and Practice in Teacher Education. Her work as a scholar, educator, and activist has centered on the problem of how to prepare and provide ongoing support for new teachers in urban public schools. Her current research projects explore the topics of adolescent literacy practices, pathways into teaching, and international teacher education. As vice chair of the Chester-Upland Education Empowerment Board, she is currently documenting multiple perspectives on change and reform in a high-poverty school district. She has published two previous books with Teachers College Press: *Listening: A Framework for Teaching Across Differences* (2003) and *School's Out!: Bridging Out-of-School Literacy with Classroom Practices* (2002, edited with Glynda Hull).